Additional praise for *Orchestrating Learning with Quality*
by David P. Langford and Barbara A. Cleary, Ph.D.

. . . not only would I buy it, I would stand on the street corner and hawk it. Orchestrating Learning with Quality is must reading. It is a book that can serve as a bible for restructuring America's schools. It supplies us with a vision, the process and tools for the schools of the future.
>—Lewis A. Rappaport
> High School Principal
> Brooklyn, New York

Other books only offer the mechanical process of applying TQM to education. This is the best book on the subject that I have read and I have learned from it.
>—Joel J. (Jim) McAbee, Superintendent
> Ware Shoals School District 51
> Ware Shoals, South Carolina

It makes a wonderful bridge for those who are interested in quality and education, but have been unable to make the connection. It is a practical education-based publication which expresses concepts within a framework that would be understood by all customers of the education system.
>—Valerie J. Gardner, Principal
> Champlain Valley Union High School
> Hinesburg, Vermont

. . . you have a powerful way of communicating the need for transformation which everyone needs to understand, because teachers alone cannot drive the transformation.
>—Maury Cotter, Director, Office of Quality Improvement
> University of Wisconsin-Madison
> Madison, Wisconsin

The way you used examples of tools in the process for adaptation and application to classrooms is excellent. I read the manuscript page by page twice! Whispering "yes, yes, I can relate to that!"
>—Vesta Dominicks, Member
> Sitka Tribal Association
> Sitka, Alaska

The book does a wonderful job of describing the quality methodology within the education context.
>—Bill Davies, Director of Staff Development
> Polk County School District
> Bartow, Florida

[I] found it to be easy to read and much more interesting than most of the books on quality. I believe it would add a great deal to the material on quality in schools which currently exists.
>—Tom Glenn
> Leander Independent School District
> Leander, Texas

In my opinion, the book fills a void for quality implementation in education. It provides the reader with the understanding of a "system of profound knowledge" for transforming the American education system.
>—Richard Haines
> Polaris Career Center
> Middlebury Height, Ohio

D0121607

Your perspective gives TQM in education a view done by the players in the game—teachers, parents, board members, students, etc. You put the "response-ability" where it should be.
>   —Paul Hedlund, Marketing Coordinator
>   Barton County Community College
>   Great Bend, Kansas

This book paints the total cultural change and implementation required to achieve any meaningful, long-lasting results. Writing style was very clear and straight-forward. Easy to read and understand. In English, as opposed to educationese. Great!
>   —Betty McCormick, Consultant
>   Austin, Texas

I have read several books on quality learning/management, but this book goes into more depth on vision, systems, and grading/self-assessment. This is a book I would refer to often for guidance and terminology.
>   —Caye Rasberry
>   Faubion Elementary School
>   Leander, Texas

The book starts in the classroom, and that has a much better chance of working "up" to trustees and superintendents than a book built the other way around. . . . Good stuff. Good style!
>   —Arnold E. Reimer, Assistant Superintendent of
>   Administration
>   St. James-Assiniboia School Division No. 2
>   Winnipeg, Manitoba, Canada

The book is very readable. Easy to understand the main ideas and the supporting evidence is excellent.
>   —Les Skillings, Teacher
>   Makawao, Hawaii

Overall, a wonderful, much-needed book. I wish it were longer, so you could elaborate more on variation, learning styles, and the basic philosophy.
>   —Anne Treviño
>   Block House Creek Elementary
>   Leander, Texas

What I liked most about your book is that I got a clear sense of what quality means in education.
>   —Kathy Wood
>   Leander Independent School District
>   Leander, Texas

I see this book offering a broad base education in the processes and theory needed to bring about changes in the system of education.
>   —Sarah Wright
>   Block House Creek Elementary
>   Leander, Texas

Orchestrating Learning with Quality

Orchestrating Learning with Quality

David P. Langford

Barbara A. Cleary, Ph.D.

ASQC Quality Press
Milwaukee, Wisconsin

Orchestrating Learning with Quality
David P. Langford and Barbara A. Cleary, Ph.D.

Library of Congress Cataloging-in-Publication Data

Langford, David P., 1957–
    Orchestrating learning with quality / David P. Langford, Barbara
A. Cleary.
      p. cm.
    Includes bibliographical references and index.
    ISBN 0-87839-321-2 (acid-free paper)
    1. Teaching. 2. Total quality management. 3. Learning.
I. Cleary, Barbara A., 1940– . II. Title.
LB1027.L249 1995
371.3'32—dc20
                                  94-45285
                                      CIP

Permission Acknowledgments

Excerpts reprinted from *Out of the Crisis*, by W. Edwards Deming by permission of MIT and W. Edwards Deming. Published by MIT, Center for Advanced Engineering Study, Cambridge, Mass. 02139. COPYRIGHT © 1986 by W. Edwards Deming.

Excerpts from *The Seven Habits of Highly Effective People*, COPYRIGHT © 1989 by Stephen R. Covey. Reprinted by permission of Simon & Schuster, Inc.

Examples and applications used by permission of
    Sidney City Schools, Sidney, Ohio, Lew Blackford, Superintendent
    Leander Independent School District, Leander, Texas, Tom Glenn, Superintendent
    The Miami Valley School, Dayton, Ohio, Thomas G. Brereton, Headmaster
    Mt. Edgecumbe High School, Sitka, Alaska, Bill Denkinger, Principal

Trademark Acknowledgment

Langford consensogram is a trademark of Langford International, Inc.

10 9 8 7 6 5 4 3 2

ISBN 0-87389-321-2

Acquisitions Editor: Susan Westergard
Project Editor: Jeanne W. Bohn

ASQC Mission: To facilitate continuous improvement and increase customer satisfaction by identifying, communicating, and promoting the use of quality principles, concepts, and technologies; and thereby be recognized throughout the world as the leading authority on, and champion for, quality.

For a free copy of the ASQC Quality Press Publications Catalog, including ASQC membership information, call 800-248-1946.

Printed in the United State of America

 Printed on acid-free recycled paper

 ASQC
Quality Press
611 East Wisconsin Avenue
Milwaukee, Wisconsin 53202

God's Child

Yellow rain slicker flashing by
Following protective stride of older sister,
The entire sky shining in your eyes,
Expectant for the promises of early school.
Backpack—requisite acccessory—flaccid with smallest content.
(No tomes or Trapper Keepers to weight your world:
Only the limp shape of patient boy-doll Fritz,
His thumbs worn from hours of nuzzling.)
Eager for school and its promise: sandbox credits, easel semesters,
Smells of colored chalk and cornstarch clay
Fat crayons stubbed by chubby grips,
And tempera in purple paint pots.

Beyond this child-garden lies another world of promises.
Endless Latin declensions and factorial confusion
Wait in bigger hallways, dark with struggle.
Now-leaden book bags carry mysteries to unravel,
Solutions themselves begetting new problems.
Anticipation turning to solemn waiting for acceptance,
Hoping only to please, seeking elusive rewards and arbitrary prizes
Of adult expectation imposed on riper imaginations.

And you wend your way, still clutching inside the tiny backpack
        of your mind
Treasures of recalled innocence, simpler friendship, the joy of learning,
Until unfettered, you again will hoist your now-lighter burden
And bound off into sunshine.

—B.A.C.

Contents

Preface

A fable

When the word about Mt. Edgecumbe High School and its pioneer use of quality theory, processes, and tools in education began to filter out of the region, educators by the hundreds made their way to Sitka, Alaska, to see what this terrific new approach to learning was like. Observing classes, talking to teachers, watching students in action, they said to each other, "This is good. This is what education is about. I want to do this in my school."

Getting back on ferries and into cars and onto airplanes, they returned to their home districts from Alaska, heartened by the successes they had seen and determined to bring change to their own schools.

And they did.

Or so they thought.

One educator introduced flexible scheduling to his school. "If students have 90-minute class periods, that will produce quality," he said.

Another, observing students working together, assigned the students in her school to do group projects. "This must be quality," she said.

Still another, remarking on the absence of ranking and grading students in one teacher's classroom, gave the good news to his own students: "No more grades!"

Each visitor, in his or her own way, thought that the spirit of quality was reflected in a particular characteristic embodied in the Mt. Edgecumbe experience.

They were wrong.

One of the difficulties in talking about quality is its complex set of interrelationships. It is not merely tools and processes. It is not outcomes. It is not portfolio assessments. It is not even continuous improvement. And attempts to produce *quality* by imitating any of these or countless other strategies are doomed to failure.

Instead, quality is a new way of seeing and thinking about the very relationship between teacher and learner. That relationship, we believe, is framed in a fundamental context that includes understandings, practices, and beliefs that enhance it and make learning happen. We call this context *quality learning,* because it is deeply rooted in fundamental principles of the total quality management philosophy, formulated in large measure by W. Edwards Deming.

It is not limited to, nor defined by, Deming's 14 points for managers, any more than it is described in a particular class-scheduling format. It is grounded in theory that embodies not only quality principles but also learning principles based on an understanding of the brain and how it functions in the learning process. It accommodates any number of what may seem to be different approaches to classroom learning, because it creates a context for that learning. When a teacher knows why he or she is using a particular technique, and places it in the context of quality learning, its relationship to learning is clear. It is not the technique but the context that produces learning.

This makes writing a book about quality a very difficult proposition. It would be nice if we could tell you some stories about those who are "doing quality," and you could imitate their successes. Our task would likewise be easier if we could describe only the fundamental principles that underpin quality learning; or if we could provide you with a tool book listing each of the statistical and problem-solving tools that can help to improve classroom learning. These tasks are left to other books, although we have drawn on them for help here and there.

Of course, we have to do some of that, or you won't know what we are talking about. In the same way that learning takes place with an undefined combination of romance for ideas with specific language and concepts related to those ideas, we must give you some combination of theoretical and practical, of concepts and tools, and of excitement and drudgery, in order to introduce you to quality.

For example, we will have to drag you, in small ways, through the this-is-where-we've-come-from stage, dreary as it may seem, in order to better understand where we are. There are those who insist that we must wake up to the dire situation of American education, and we agree. At the same time, we will share some of the successes we know about and have experienced. And we'll give you a few tools.

The impact of quality does not lie in any cookbook approach to change. Instead, it is embodied in the remarks of teachers who say they feel "released, and free to think," and in the superintendent's saying to a principal who has approached him with a plan or idea, "What's stopping you from doing it?" The impact of quality is found in teachers who turn to their students for learning, in students who become facilitators of their own and others' learning, in administrators who say, "This concept has changed my life," and in leaders who say "I've gained so much by letting go."

If we were to create a you-are-here map to this book, it might look something like this.

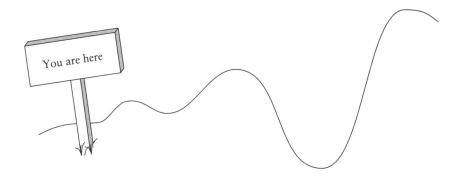

It may not look like what you think of when you hear the term *continuous improvement*, which implies a steady, upward path. Instead, it has its struggles with the recognition that our schools are flawed, with the difficult matter of how to begin, and with understanding statistical concepts related to variation and control charts. The book alone cannot solve your educational problems, nor will it provide the recipe for which you are looking. Instead it will start you on a path that may be steep and difficult. Like quality learning, the path may not be easy. We hope that it will challenge you to think in new ways and to see the learning process in a new light.

When that happens, you will know it.

We wrote this book primarily for educators in the broadest sense of that word. Our operational definition of *educator* is one who learns, facilitates learning, supports the learning process, pays for learning, or receives the benefit of someone's learning. This would include students and teachers, administrators and school board members, school staff members, parents, taxpayers, college professors and decision-makers (especially those in schools of education), and employers. The book's overview of education and how schools can be improved is derived from our understanding of the learning process itself, rather than from the perspective of the limitations that school systems face.

Those who consider themselves quality professionals are among our customers as well; their experiences in recognizing that all processes benefit from the theory, process, and tools of quality are critical to changing the paradigm that service processes are somehow unique and not susceptible to the same improvement as those in manufacturing. Those in health care and other people-centered and service-oriented systems provide clear testimony that processes can be approached in new ways to benefit all.

Our examples are drawn from our own experiences in the classroom and as consultants to others' classrooms and schools. They are real examples, though we have not always provided names. Our own teaching experiences have been in inner-city junior high school classrooms, suburban public schools, an independent college preparatory school, university classrooms, a parochial elementary school, and a public boarding school primarily for ethnic minorities. Between us, we have taught in schools in Colorado, Montana, Alaska, Nebraska, Connecticut, New Jersey, and Ohio. While our teaching experiences have been primarily in the upper grades, we have seen how elementary classrooms are using the theory, process, and tools of quality to improve their processes, and have reported some of these successes in this book.

The book approaches quality and learning from the point of view of theory (understanding systems, variation, customers, and learning itself); process (the plan-do-study-act approach to improvement, using alternative assessment practices, and developing team processes); and tools (illustrating some of the tools to use along the way—not for their own sake, but when they are fundamental to the process). Our purpose is to support learning—yours and those whom you influence—by providing examples wherever we can. These examples are usually just snippets of applications, since our purpose is to give a bigger picture rather than a step-by-step walk-through of the entire improvement process. In some cases, the examples are drawn from classrooms in school districts that have no commitment or interest in quality but where teachers are nonetheless using the theory, process, and tools to bring about their own improvement.

As hitchhikers on the information highway, we would have liked to create this discussion in the form of interactive communication rather than as a book, to facilitate exchange of ideas, and to record new classroom experiences. We hope that you will approach it in this way, as a dialogue to begin discussion rather than as a finished rendition.

And we will look forward to continuing the dialogue.

—David P. Langford
—Barbara A. Cleary, Ph.D.

Acknowledgments

We acknowledge those who have supported us along the path, especially those who read the manuscript at various stages and gave suggestions for improvement and encouragement of effort.

Barbara thanks those at PQ Systems, Inc., especially learning partners Sally Duncan, Steve Kreitzer, and Janet Strawn; as well as all those who reviewed the manuscript: Superintendent Robert Kattman; Harry Forsha; The Miami Valley School Headmaster Tom Brereton who supported the journey; Sean, Tim, Matt, and Dennis for their stories and their faith; and especially Mike, who helped identify the path in the first place.

David thanks the following people who reviewed the manuscript and provided insightful, valuable feedback and support: Monta Akin, Carlos Arce, Joel Barker, Maury Cotter, Bill Davies, Lloyd Dobyns, Vesta Dominicks, Buck Evans, Doris Fassino, Val Gardner, Tom Glenn, Jay Gould, Richard Haines, Paul Hedlund, Susie Huggins, John Hutcherson, Jim McAbee, Betty McCormick, Pat O'Brien, Caye Rasberry, Arnold Reimer, Sue Reynard, Les Skillings, Anne Treviño, Myron Tribus, Kathy Wood, Robert Wood, and Sarah Wright.

David sends a special thanks to the entire Leander Independent School District in Leander, Texas. It has been a continual source of learning and inspiration.

Chapter 1

A New Way of Thinking

*In each new epoch—perhaps every generation, or even
every few years, if the conditions in which we live
change that rapidly—it becomes necessary to rethink
and reformulate what it takes to establish autonomy in
consciousness.*

—Mihaly Csikszentmihalyi
Flow: The Psychology of Optimal Experience

On the first day of school, a high school journalism class enters the publication room expecting a syllabus, a list of assignments, and rules for behavior in the classroom. Students sit at tables, which have been moved together, roundtable style, ready to take notes about what the teacher wants from them.

Instead, the teacher-facilitator passes out pads of yellow sticky notes and asks students to indicate their expectations for the course. "What do you need to get out of the class this term?" she asks. Then she allows them time to record their ideas, one per note. At first, the students glance around, trying to see what others are doing, attempting to determine what they're supposed to write, but then their heads go down and their pens are busy. As leader of the process, the teacher may elect not to participate in it, but it is important that if she does not contribute ideas to the note-taking process, students understand the facilitator role as external to that process.

After they have had time to record their ideas, the teacher asks the students to stand up and walk around the table, looking at each other's ideas. Then, without discussion, the students try to group similar ideas together. Soon, the sticky notes are grouped in small batches across the table. One student takes them all and sticks them to the wall so everyone can clearly see them. There is further adjustment, followed by an exercise identifying each group.

After the groupings are complete, the teacher suggests that the students name each batch of ideas with a header to identify it. She is using a tool—the affinity diagram—to help students organize their thinking. The emphasis, however, is not on learning the tool, but on identifying their needs for the term.

1

The groupings as they were actually conceived by this class are reflected in Figure 1.1. In that diagram, the headings had not yet been created, but it is clear that the ideas fall into a number of groups with similarities: learning to conduct interviews, for example, or improving skills of page layout and design.

After they have had a chance to study what they have written, and to revise the groupings as appropriate, the teacher asks the students if they think it will be possible to meet these expectations for the term. Heads nod. "How can we accomplish this?" she asks. Students begin to identify ways in which each group of expectations can be met. For "learn how to do an interview," for example, they brainstorm and come up with "practice interviews on each other," "learn what questions to ask," "read about interview strategies in the textbook," "watch tapes of good news interviews from television," and other strategies to accomplish the goal of developing skills in this area. The teacher participates, occasionally offering her suggestions (for example, "Does anyone know a newspaper reporter?").

After such strategies have been generated for each of the groupings, the teacher stands back, nods, and says, "Well, there's our course!"

After this scenario had taken place in a classroom in Ohio, the teacher commented to a colleague, "You know, if I had sat down to plan the course and determine assignments, I would have come up with a lot of the same things for them to do. But they would have been *my* strategies. Instead, they're *theirs*. The students own the learning themselves. And they're more ambitious than I would have dared to be."

New ways of thinking about learning

Quality learning is a new way of thinking about education—one that will help students and teachers take responsibility for their own learning, give them tools to solve problems, and provide the means to understand how specific learning processes fit into a larger system of learning with certain predictable characteristics.

While other strategies practiced by teachers contribute to these aims, quality learning represents a way to orchestrate specific strategies and to bring them together to create a "learning organization" (Senge 1990). It is important to understand that this is not another program, or strategy, but a way of seeing, so that all programs and strategies used in a classroom are understood in terms of their contribution to the aim of the system that is in place.

Students—until their native love of learning has been quashed—know something about their own learning needs. Even a young child going to school for the first time will articulate a need to learn to read

What I need to learn in this course

Get involved with school newspaper.

Create weekly newsletter for school.

Learn how to do layout.

Improve involvement with newspaper staff.

Work cooperatively with the class to produce a quality bulletin.

Improve my spelling.

Improve and work on a newspaper.

Be able to provide current news to everyone in a newsletter format.

Work on meeting deadlines.

Become knowledgeable enough to judge the quality of writing in newspapers.

Work on interviewing skills.

Improve my skills for gathering important information.

Learn how to give effective interviews.

Learn how to get to the point.

Be able to judge the quality of articles I read in papers and magazines.

Improve interviewing skills.

Improve my thoughts and express myself better in writing.

Improve my editing ability.

Do research and form an educated opinion on issues important to me.

Learn to be more creative in the selection of stories.

Expand ideas for angles and topics for stories.

Learn how to make boring facts exciting.

Learn to edit.

Improve computer layout skills.

Learn to easily identify possible stories to write.

Learn more about using the computer for journalism.

Study all forms of journalism including print and broadcast.

Learn how to write qualitatively.

Learn how to better use a computer.

Learn about different types of journalism.

Improve the quality of articles I write.

Learn to use computer software.

Learn basics about journalism.

Learn a new approach to expository writing.

Learn more about computers.

Learn about journalism in general.

Improve writing.

Improve my computer skills.

Learn about the process of publishing a newspaper.

Improve writing skills.

Learn to use drawing software.

Improve my writing.

Learn the Macintosh system.

Find out if this is something I want to do in college.

Develop better writing skills.

Learn to do computer layouts.

Learn about journalism as a career.

Improve writing quality.

Learn how to work on the computer.

Learn about professions in journalism.

Learn how to write articles.

Learn how to use the computer.

Learn how to write articles properly.

Learn page layout software.

Acquire new skills in writing.

Experiment with computer graphics.

Have fun!

Improve my writing of news rather than features, to extend my journalistic range.

Have fun and learn!

Figure 1.1: Affinity diagram (grouped, but not yet labeled).

or write or create drawings. When schools underestimate this ability to identify needs and develop strategies for satisfying them, the result is the teacher-directed, meaningless process that is endemic to many classrooms. When the child's interest in his or her own learning is fostered, the results are astounding.

While this observation may seem basic to some, it is clear that the educational system that has been designed to serve the learning needs of generations of Americans has somehow lost its focus. What is needed is a reexamination of the purpose of schools and a rededication to constancy in serving this purpose.

Schools reflect—for good or ill—the society in which they exist. Unfortunately, the educational system of the twentieth century is one that was designed for the society of the nineteenth. In the same way that American industry has awakened to the new challenges of the global economy, changing customer bases, and acute competition, education must identify the needs of the twenty-first century and move toward meeting those needs.

Quality learning offers a way to do this. The methods of W. Edwards Deming (1986) and other contributors to what has become known as *total quality management* (TQM) (though Deming himself never used that term) are now widely recognized and practiced by organizations throughout the United States. Organizations that have adopted ways to improve the quality of their products and services find themselves able to thrive in an increasingly competitive world market. A systems perspective and Deming's system of profound knowledge have provided a guideline for new ways of thinking in organizations that face, in effect, a new world situation. This new paradigm represented in Deming's thinking—a new model for operating organizations—builds on a sensitivity to those who are identified as the customers of the organization. Customers are those who receive the benefit of the products or services, both inside and outside the organization. The entire organization must share a common vision of its customers and how it can best serve them. While other tenets of the Deming philosophy are critical to quality management's success, understanding the customer—the one who benefits from products or services generated by an organization—is a keystone to these tenets.

The legendary story of a buggy whip manufacturer illustrates the need for understanding the organization in terms of its customers. Responding to steadily lagging sales, the buggy whip maker tried to reverse the decline by working even harder to improve the quality of his products. Devoting all of his energy to making better buggy whips, he did indeed see the quality of the product improve. As his workforce produced increasingly better products, however, sales continued to drop. The manufacturer focused on making improved buggy whips, confident that high-quality products would sell themselves. Finally driven to bankruptcy because no one was buying his product, the manufacturer realized that while he had been concentrating on improving his whips, the horse-drawn buggy had been replaced by the automobile. The world had changed, and so had the expectations of his customers. If organizations are to improve, they must do far more than work harder at what they are already doing. In the same way, schools can continue to improve their facilities, and even their test scores. But if they are not preparing their students for the next century, these piecemeal improvements are meaningless.

A new management for quality

Quality management places an emphasis not only on developing constancy of purpose in understanding customers' needs, but also on eliminating harmful practices (such as ranking and rating people in the organization); working with support groups to create a sense of trust and partnership; providing ongoing training for everyone in the organization; restoring pride of workmanship by removing barriers within the organization; driving out fear; and instituting leadership throughout the organization. Because this approach represents a new way of thinking, it is not easily adopted like a single program in an organization. Instead, it demands a willingness to rethink fundamental ways of doing business. With so much discussion of restructuring schools, the time is ripe to consider adopting a new way of thinking in education. Management theorist Peter Vaill (1989, 14) points out that even though our culture is evolving in turbulent new ways with new relationships among organizations, "old ways of talking about these new forms hang on and cloud our thinking."

Throughout this country, many organizations that are pursuing continuous improvement practices through TQM have experienced dramatic improvements in the quality of their products and services. Workers find a new sense of joy in their work and managers find that they must no longer merely supervise but can truly lead. Other outcomes include a greater sense of responsibility for the success of the organization, diminished absenteeism and turnover among employees, and higher levels of cooperation with suppliers and even among competitors to produce higher-quality products and services.

While enlightened representatives of American industry enjoy these positive outcomes and their customers find delight in improved products and services, a much less positive picture emerges when America's system of education is examined. Schools have continued to provide the same products and services that made them successful a generation ago. Like the buggy whip manufacturer, those who manage the nation's schools have failed to focus on a changing world by demanding different outcomes from the educational system. Continuing to pursue the same course while expecting different outcomes defies any kind of logic.

Our nineteenth-century outlook

Public schools often reflect social and economic trends in the United States. To respond to industrialization, for example, schools prepared students to take their place in an automated workforce. In addition, schools themselves adopted the industrial model as a guide for effective education. A factory approach to advancing students and rewarding them with grades emphasized output and productivity, mimicking the reward system of factories—but with grades, extra credit, and free time instead of salary, bonuses, and benefits. Looking back 50 years, much of what we know as everyday life would be different, such as homes, computers, video games, air transportation, and shopping malls. One of the few aspects of life that would reflect very little change and would be clearly recognizable to young people would be the schools, which operate in many of the same ways today as they did half a century ago.

In the classroom, nineteenth-century approaches to educational theory based on that century's new interest in science—abetted by Frederick Taylor's emphasis on organizational theory and Henry Ford's applications in the factories of this century—are largely responsible for the ways in which classroom learning takes place—the "doing to" method of education. The emphasis on individual effort and on ranking students with respect to individual scores often reinforced their sense that they had not learned much in school. This emphasis replaced much more spontaneous and informal approaches to education that had characterized earlier classrooms. A flurry of technological inventiveness had convinced many that the scientific method represented not only a new way of thinking, but perhaps the solution to all the world's problems. Although writers like Nathaniel Hawthorne warned against an overreliance on science, the American public remained intrigued by the promises it whispered.

The nineteenth century shaped our public schools in a variety of ways. Influenced by the new infatuation with scientific method and technology, educators and planners imposed these methods on schools. And of course, those schools worked. They were well suited to the society that they served. This was a society in which young people could expect to enter the workforce in the same area where they had grown up and could anticipate lifestyles roughly equivalent to those of their parents.

Schools were expected to prepare young people to take their places in an increasingly industrialized society and to assume jobs in organizations where they could be counted on to follow directions provided by a top-down leadership style. The best schools emphasized authority, discipline, and student submission to teachers' directions about learning.

Looking and thinking ahead

But times have changed. The world is a different place now than it was even a decade ago. Students are no longer destined for work on assembly lines; their family lives are different, often following nontraditional and even dysfunctional patterns; electronic media have brought the rest of the world into our living rooms and onto our computer screens. Simultaneously, there is a well-documented crisis in education; virtually no one is satisfied with the job that the schools are doing. Simply put, current educational systems are not meeting the needs of society of this decade—the customer—nor are they addressing the requirements of the next century. A paradox lies in the fact that when large gatherings of people are asked if they think education needs to be changed, nearly all of them raise their hands. Yet, in surveys such as that taken by Phi Delta Kappa, more than two-thirds of respondents invariably give their own children's schools grades of *A* or *B* (Gallup and Elam 1988). Either grade inflation has affected these responses, or there is widespread public unwillingness to acknowledge the need for dramatic change. In either case, the situation is alarming.

   In addressing the needs of the future, it is clear that changes will have to be made in education in the same ways that industry has had to make changes in the way it operates. If education continues to do what it is doing, schools will continue to produce what they are producing, no matter how hard they work at it. Just like the buggy whip manufacturer, a society that continues to invest in obsolete educational methods will not be able to meet the needs of an altered world. To survive the current crisis, all organizations, including schools, must focus on the quality of their services and products. Those that fail to meet the demands for quality will not survive (Glasser 1990).

   When schools do not understand their purpose and the needs of their customers, they are not equipped to adapt to changing needs or to meet new requirements. For example, for decades one of the major thrusts of education was that of teaching students how to acquire information. Young people were introduced to library research skills, taught about note cards and bibliography entries, encouraged to use a variety of source materials, and from high school through graduate school were assigned research papers that were designed to demonstrate their ability to track down information. Piles of note cards have attested to students' ability to locate their sources and dutifully record the germane parts.

New skills, new adaptations

These skills are certainly important ones. Understanding the use of tools is fundamental to the acquisition of any kind of knowledge, whether practical or theoretical. In an age of information, however, when students can already access the entire Library of Congress by means of computers, and where research in the professions is conducted by electronics that streamline the process and provide thousands of sources that are otherwise unavailable except in highly specialized libraries, one wonders how useful the acquisition skills will be to this generation. Once students are able to confront the Library of Congress in one fell swoop, it is certainly not the how-to-collect-information skills that are fundamental to success, but the what-to-do-with-all-this-information skills. Schools must address use of the tools in light of the changing environment that graduating students will increasingly face. If young people know only note-card technology without its connection to the larger purpose, why in the world would one expect those students to find meaning or joy in the task of collecting note cards? And yet year after year in schools across this nation, students submit mountains of note cards for teachers to evaluate.

When the world changes around us, we are slow to internalize that change even when we accept it intellectually. It was one thing for early explorers to demonstrate unequivocally that the earth was not flat. It was another for their contemporaries to internalize that information, and actually remember as they looked at the horizon, that there was more than that apparent line. They had to keep reminding themselves—even after they knew that the earth was round. So, too, we need to keep reminding ourselves that our students can do their homework with electronic mail, or can create an interactive computer program that catalogs their baseball card collections. In many ways, they are ahead of their teachers, who can become their co-learners in this new wonderland.

Unless educators understand what is happening in the world around them, they cannot provide entirely appropriate preparation for their graduates. Technology can open countless new doors to the fundamentals, even in the learning process. Schools resisted the use of the handheld calculator in the classroom long after every kid on the block owned a little solar-powered calculator shaped like a bunny or a miniature circus tent. This amazing technological breakthrough had become a Christmas stocking stuffer long before the trigonometry class abandoned its slide rules. Teachers were assiduously preparing their students for the nineteenth century, even while using calculators to balance their own checkbooks.

The big picture and joy in learning

How are teachers to understand the needs of their students? Only by keeping their eyes on the large world in which young people will find themselves. That is not to say that all education must be relevant in the 1970s sense of practical and immediately applicable to a work environment, nor that schools need to respond to every shift in the educational winds. But when students and teachers at all levels realize the value of the lifetime thinking skills that will enable them to address and solve problems in both their academic and work lives, then real relevance will be a source of inspiration for both teachers and students. Excitement for learning—what Deming calls joy in work—will replace the sense of despair that has imbued schools.

We know the enthusiasm of the youngster beginning school. The four-year-old girl runs home from preschool clutching a large piece of paper rolled into a tube with masking tape binding its seam. She can hardly wait to show it to her parents. As she pulls off the tape and frees the sheet—entirely covered with purple, bold strokes of yellow and red slashing across the bright background and adding texture with layered globs of paint—she assesses it unabashedly, "It's my painting and it's beautiful."

This scene, repeated countless times with each child who begins school in this country, contrasts sharply with that of the sullen high school student, embarrassed about displaying his or her work or so ashamed of poor quality work that it is never even submitted, much less shared with parents. This scene is also repeated endlessly in our nation's schools. Indeed, when high school students were asked in the mid-1980s what they liked best about school, the answer given most frequently was "nothing." (Wold 1994)

What happens to joy in learning and pride in workmanship like that which consumes the four-year-old? Recognize the pattern: That young child who can hardly wait to get to school becomes the jaded adolescent looking for ways to get by. At what point in the educational process do young people stop learning for the sake of pure joy and pride in their own creativity, and begin playing the game of working only to levels that will satisfy their parents and teachers?

The very purpose of the educational system is to cultivate a sense of joy in learning so that students will be equipped by their educations to continue that process throughout life, even in the face of change. Yet it is this very love of learning that is missing from many schools.

Changing the tire

Teachers have often felt there must be a way to sustain or restore exuberance for learning in all children. But teachers have sensed that the solutions are outside their control because they are so complex and far-reaching. Consequently, they go on doing the same things in their classrooms because they don't know what else to do. In the meantime, education is being asked to take on more tasks. In the frenzy of pursuing additional goals and documenting increasing objectives, we really do not have time to analyze the large system and think deeply about changing it. It's like trying to change a flat tire on a car that's moving 60 miles an hour down the highway. Unfortunately, by not addressing our problems at a systemic level, we may not only damage the tire further, but we may also lose the whole car.

While we somehow understand that there is something wrong with the educational process, it is hard to understand exactly what it is. As a result, we frequently blame the child ("He's just lazy." "She was always a little slow."); or the parents ("It's a broken home, you know." "The father's unemployed."); or, of course, the teachers and their lack of preparation, or the school board's misplaced priorities. We rarely analyze the system of education itself to see if there are ways in which that system fails its learners. But evidence that success in school is related to a cyclical pattern of problems in society is dramatic. Carnevale, Gainer, and Meltzer (1988) investigated the educational backgrounds of adults who have patterns of low success in society. They found that 68 percent of those arrested, 85 percent of unwed mothers, 79 percent of welfare dependents, and 72 percent of the unemployed did poorly in school. Many of the problems that people consider to be critical challenges of the 1990s—crime, violence, foreign competition, and voter apathy, for example—are directly related to inadequately developed skills of problem solving and critical thinking.

Where there is joy in learning, an independent learner will emerge. Where there is coercion and competition, test results may go up but independent learning is diminished. It is possible to tweak the system to produce higher test scores, better grades, lower dropout rates, or other indicators of good schools. If enough resources are devoted to a single area, that area can certainly be improved. The entire system, however, must be changed to bring about the quality in education that is marked by students who are eager to learn and willing to take responsibility for that learning. As quality learning principles demonstrate, fixing parts of the system will never improve the system itself.

In order for schools to determine their course, educators might profitably look at the organizations that are actually producing high quality in their goods and services, such as the manufacturing and service industries that have adopted new methods of managing for quality. But educators should be cautioned to examine the large picture as they analyze what's happening in these organizations. It is always easy to find examples where people are doing something right—improving one aspect of an organization or a school or a classroom procedure. Behind every Teacher of the Year or National Excellence in Education award is recognition of this fact. What will be demanded, however, is an understanding of how the entire system, not just its individual parts, can be improved enough to assure its survival and to guarantee high-quality outcomes. For this to happen, it is not enough to emulate examples of improvement in component parts of a system. It will, in fact, be destructive to the eventual outcome to rely on this kind of piecemeal improvement. What is demanded is knowledge about how systems operate and how they can be improved as systems. As will be demonstrated in chapter 2, this kind of knowledge is fundamental to the success of change efforts. Clearly this cannot happen overnight, for quality improvement is a long-term proposition.

Reform without meaning

Contributing to the failure of schools these days is not the schools themselves, but the plethora of educational reform movements that have been marshaled to change education. In this parade of failures, school districts have leaped from what was known as progressive education some 40 years ago, to trendy interests in open classrooms, individually guided education, tracking and then not tracking, programs for the gifted, specialized methods of teaching reading or math, and the ill-defined, back-to-the-basics clamor of the 1980s. Such approaches often reflect a specific public outcry about schools, and thus they tend to come and go as the public's attention shifts. A lack of system thinking seems endemic both to current practice and public perception.

It is clear that some of these methods and movements have failed because of underfunding and overpromising rather than from fundamental flaws in their thinking; they have also fallen victim to poor training on the part of those using them, political pressure from all sides, and in some cases lack of understanding of human development needs entirely. The most far-reaching and important reason for the failure of any single educational reform idea, however, is ultimately a lack of identifying with educational purpose—the big "so what?"—not just of math programs or arts education, but of schools in general. It is true that each change may identify a problem area and provide a solution. But almost without fail, these reforms fail to address the largest context of education, the very purpose of schools. If there is no larger theory to support a specific technique, the technique—no matter how positive its results may be in the short term—is doomed to failure. Some very good ideas have been victims of this fact; teachers who have tried out a variety of excellent classroom techniques know this well. For example, cooperative learning—a useful approach—has no meaning when students simply break into small groups without knowing why.

A view of the big picture means that changes can be understood as they affect the entire system rather than only a small part of it. As we will see, by identifying the processes that are involved in a system and that contribute to it, and by understanding the theory of variation in systems, an organization can determine where change must be made and identify when change represents only a kind of tampering, without the data to know what to change. It is a truth of organizations as well as of good medical practice that no matter how many external bandages are applied, systemic dysfunction will not go away unless fundamental changes are made that affect the entire system.

When schools respond to the public outcry about education by implementing short-term and therefore ill-advised changes without understanding their effect on the entire system, such change is doomed to failure and the schools themselves will face a future even more dismal than that which they envision now. "We tried that already" is the death knell for improvement efforts. So how can change come about?

Industry lessons

Fortunately, the educational system can look to its counterparts in industry for some trial-and-error lessons as well as for inspiration in improving the quality of schools. The issues are related to leadership at all levels; to systems thinking and understanding of variation within systems; to an understanding of customers; and to an emphasis on teamwork and developing intrinsically motivating learning environments rather than to competition at all organizational levels. The time has come for a new kind of leadership that is responsive to the challenges of education and that understands the century in which students will live and work.

Fundamentally, the improvement process known as *quality learning* involves understanding the systems within which problems are addressed, rather than solving these problems in isolation. Its emphasis on the big picture creates an atmosphere in which the issue is one of making changes to a system based on understanding its fundamental variation, rather than blaming individuals for failures in the system. Management philosophies derived from TQM support sound educational practices and amplify their positive effects.

For schools, this kind of understanding of systems should not represent as great a reach as it does for some industries. The language of schools as systems is already in place; it is critical that they begin to function as systems. Fundamental characteristics of systems apply to school districts as well as to individual classrooms, but these characteristics must be fully understood. Examining the precedents in American industry, which has understood its own crisis for a number of years, can be instructive if schools are willing to listen.

Of course, schools do not operate within the same profit framework that businesses must, and educational professionals are often offended when their institutions are described in business terms. The American Association of School Administrators leader Lewis A. Rhodes (1990, 24) suggests that "even the most enlightened school reformers deride the industrial model when applied to schooling." To educators, terms derived from commerce suggest material production and factory standards. (The irony that our public schools were originally designed after the factory model of the nineteenth century is not to be missed.) Even at policy-making levels, educators are suspicious of the involvement of American business in their profession (Weisman 1991). This diffidence about being compared to businesses may be generated by the fact that education, as a recession-proof industry, does not find itself in need of customers, nor do educators think in these terms as they prepare budgets. Current experiments create private schools out of public by turning them over to external, entrepreneurial organizations rather than by schools' adopting the methods of business.

Some of the language of business applies in a real sense to our schools; it is clear that there are costs both known and unknowable to the continued operation of poor-quality schools. Every student who drops out of school loses an estimated $240,000 in lifetime earnings. This represents $228 billion in lost lifetime earnings for each high school graduating class nationally. Associated costs include $68 billion in lost tax revenues annually; $41 billion in welfare programs; and $3 billion annually in expenditures to fight crime (Carnevale, Gainer, and Meltzer 1988).

We think of education as an investment in the future. But because our schools are not providing appropriate skills for the future, it is often the businesses themselves that are making the investment in learning. Industry's cost for retraining is substantial, and businesses are quick to point out that this investment is not just in so-called vocational skills, but in the fundamentals of reading, computing, and writing as well. In 1989, industry for the first time spent more money on training and education than did post-secondary schools. An Ohio manufacturer of instrumentation devices undertook a major education program for its employees, including reading, writing, and math basics, as well as the team skills employees need to succeed in the company's environment. A major consultant in statistical process control acknowledges that much of his consulting time is spent on remedial statistical education, even among managers of *FORTUNE* 500 organizations. "It's as bad in the executive suites as it is on the factory floor," he says (Schrage 1991). The traditional high school math curriculum, for example, does not include statistics, and yet an understanding of statistics holds the key to improvement in all kinds of processes—from manufacturing widgets to running a university to learning a new skill. It is applicable to the sports world: understanding the theory of variation in engine operation could save thousands of dollars spent on testing race cars. Great composers understand the beauty that lies in variation of musical themes, and orchestras benefit from understanding variability in performances as well as in audiences. If business is to bear much of the cost of the schools' inadequacy, commerce might be looked to for approaches to the amelioration of these inadequacies.

From coercion to cooperation

In another shift, one of the fundamental changes that has taken place in American industry is its emphasis on cooperation rather than competition within organizations. Workers, trained in problem-solving skills, address improvement projects that affect not only their own areas but also the organization as a whole. Cooperation with suppliers and even competitors in the marketplace will bring about a new customer focus in organizations' products and services. Thus, the graduates of our schools will be required to have skills in team problem solving and group planning, rather than those of merely following orders, as an earlier generation of workers might have. As will be seen in later chapters, these skills can be fostered in an environment of quality learning.

The emphasis on collaboration and cooperation can be found in recent educational language, notably that of *cooperative learning,* which focuses on the benefits of teamwork in learning. Ideally, the element of competition does not exist between teams; instead the classroom is a place where students learn in small groups rather than only on their own, and where teams of students work together to enhance the performance of all.

To understand the relationship between the schools and the society that receives their graduates, and to realize the impact that one has on the other, it is also useful to examine the management style of most educational systems. To become a learning organization, a school must change its focus from "doing to" the student to one of "doing with." It is only with this emphasis that students will take responsibility for their own learning and regain their sense of joy in the learning process. But first, management structures in school organizations must be examined to determine the ways in which managers of school systems "do to" their employees (including teachers) rather than "doing with" them to develop comprehensive improvement efforts in their schools.

The demand at all levels for reforms in education tempts those responsible for schools to latch on to a variety of projects and programs, frenetically putting into place so-called solutions to complex problems that are often not at all amenable to such simple approaches, and, in the long run, undermining the possibility of positive change entirely. This approach is not new, however, nor is it restricted to education. The business community—with its parade of attempts to change and improve—has long practiced such short-term thinking. In fact, the need to do something—the quicker the better—is endemic to American life. Leaping into the quickest apparent solution not only fails to address problems, but such an approach is also responsible for the cynicism, poor worker morale, and the inability to progress that are characteristic of many organizations. The long-term negative effects far outweigh short-term benefits.

The framework within which visionary thinking about reform is translated into action demands the use of important tools—those that have already been put to use in the context of American industry and are eminently consistent with sound educational philosophies. We might have the clearest vision in the world, but unless we understand the processes that will help to bring that vision to reality, it does not matter how hard we try or how purely we are motivated—it just won't happen.

Moving toward systems

Quality learning, then, offers a new way to see the system of education. It provides ways to focus on student learning, enhancing students' abilities to take responsibility for that learning, and using what we know about the learning process to facilitate learning. It offers a framework within which educators, parents, and community members can understand and respond to changing demographics, expanding technology, and diminishing resources.

By designing systems to serve the needs of the schools' customers, and by understanding the characteristics of systems and reducing the variation that takes place within them, the fundamentals of quality learning will help to establish an atmosphere where genuine leadership can work cooperatively with all those who are part of the educational system. What will ensue is a reiteration of the fundamental purpose of the system, a constant revisiting of how processes support the system of learning, and ultimately, a vastly improved educational program for our nation.

Notes

Carnevale, A. P., L. J. Gainer, and A. S. Meltzer. 1988. *Workplace basics: The skills employers want.* Washington, D.C.: American Society for Training and Development and U.S. Department of Labor.

Csikszentmihalyi, Mihaly. 1990. *Flow: Psychology of optimal experience.* New York: Harper & Row.

Deming, W. Edwards. 1986. *Out of the crisis.* Cambridge, Mass.: MIT Center for Advanced Engineering Study.

Gallup, Alec M., and Stanley M. Elam. 1988. Twentieth annual Gallup poll of public attitudes toward public schools. 1988. *Phi Delta Kappan* (September): 33–34.

Glasser, William. 1990. The quality school: What motivates the ants. *Phi Delta Kappan* (February): 425–435.

Rhodes, L. A. 1990. Why quality is within our grasp . . . If we reach. *The School Administrator* 47, no. 10:31–34.

Schrage, Michael. 1991. If statistics are the key to quality, our students need some chance encounters. *Washington Post*, 15 March.

Senge, Peter. 1990. *The fifth discipline: The art and practice of the learning organization.* New York: Doubleday.

Vaill, Peter. 1989. *Managing as a performing art.* San Francisco: Jossey-Bass.

Weisman, Jonathan. 1991. Educators watch with a wary eye as business gains policy muscle. *Education Week*, 31 July, 1.

Wold, Ronald A. 1994. The quiet crisis. *Teacher Magazine* (January): 3.

Chapter 2

Understanding Systems

*Education might well be defined as knowing the story
of the universe, of the planet Earth, of life systems, and
of consciousness, all as a single story, and recognizing
the human role in the story. The primary purpose of
education should be to enable individual humans to
fulfill their proper role in this larger pattern of
meaning. We can understand this role in the Great
Story only if we know the story in its full dimensions.*

—Brian Swimme and Thomas Berry,
The Universe Story

Images of quality learning approaches in schools are everywhere. Hints
of their successes are provided in stories about third graders charting
their spelling progress, groups of teachers at a high school in Kentucky
working together to solve the problem of classroom interruptions, and
superintendents inviting their counterparts in industry to see quality
learning in action in their schools.

But it has been difficult to get our arms around what the total quality approach really means when it is applied to education. A Sufi story
recounts four curious citizens who were sent to find out the nature of
the elephant that had been stabled near their town. No one in the town
had ever seen an elephant before, and the four were dispatched to determine the animal's nature in the dim light that the stable afforded. The
first, feeling the elephant's trunk, described the animal as a "thick hose-
like creature;" another, experiencing the leg and ear, defined the animal
in terms of "a living pillar" and a fan. Each observer defined the animal
differently (Shah 1964).

Similarly, a definition of quality learning that addresses only its
parts cannot convey even an outline of its nature. It is important to
come to terms with what makes it what it is, and to understand how it

works. This chapter will begin to describe the "elephant" by identifying not only its parts, but what makes it work as a system.

Looking at the whole elephant

As we have seen, many educational reforms have not worked, because they address only symptoms or because they offer hope for improvement of only one aspect of education. What is most fundamental to quality learning is the understanding of education as a system that can be improved rather than as a series of unrelated subsystems that just happen to occupy the same general space. Piecemeal approaches have not worked; the integrity of a system must be acknowledged and utilized. Many now agree that change in learning organizations must be systemic.

Before the possibilities for systemic change can be seen, it is essential to understand the nature of a system and how its parts work together in a purposeful, integrated way. For example, Senge (1990) points out that the system of a rainstorm can be understood only by contemplating the whole, not any individual part of the storm pattern. The interrelationships among the parts and the unity of the whole are what characterize systems.

It is easy to find examples of systems that do *not* work in this way. A high school history teacher laments, "My students won't get past World War II again this year." An advanced placement preparation course skips several chapters in students' textbooks, since the test won't cover that material. An advanced algebra teacher complains that her students have forgotten any earlier algebra they may have been exposed to. And junior-year English students protest, "But we've never heard of dangling modifiers before!"

At the high school level in particular, students are often protected from understanding how various disciplines support each other. They see their learning in the same way they see their notebooks: separate sections for math, history, and English, with ideas presented by a teacher or book, dutifully recorded, evaluated with respect to their relevance to a test, and then forgotten.

When students learn in artificial segments, and when their understanding is fragmented by careful separation of disciplines, prescribed course content, and the daily pressures of the school year, it's no wonder that students forget what they've learned from one year to another, that they have little understanding of how history is related to art and literature, and that they see little relevance in their educational program. The world, as Ackoff and Emery (1972) emphasize, does not come in a neat, disciplinary form. Phenomena are not "physical," "chemical," "biological," and so on. The disciplines, such as the scientific disciplines of chemistry and biology, are ways in which we study phenomena; they are not the phenomena themselves. A "filing system of knowledge," the organization of what we know about the world is not to be confused with the world itself.

Systems as integrated processes

Students often do not experience learning in school as an integrated process that will help them to lead productive and rewarding lives. In fact, they rarely think about the purpose of even going to school, for it all seems so short term. The idea, after all, is to take whatever program is necessary in order to graduate, or to do only what is required. Like the adult who works for an entire lifetime just to be able to retire, a student's goal is often just to get out of the system. In short, students do not see their education as a *process,* a series of events that support a larger system with its own *purpose.* Nor do they see themselves as learning within a system designed to bring about some shared end, or as being responsible for their role in that system.

At the same time, teachers themselves often fail to understand their roles within such a system. Their sense of purpose may derive only from their own particular processes: to help students learn to read, to master French verbs, and to write clear thesis statements. Understanding the purpose of school is sometimes limited by the bounds of teachers' own disciplines or processes. Disciplinary teaching can become a way of seeing the world.

Without a sense of the school as a system, each of these individual processes lacks relationships to other processes. Students often feel overwhelmed by the fragmented pieces of education that are their experience. If education were indeed viewed as a system, such fragmentation would not ensue, for the processes that make up the system would be moving in the same direction. Once the elephant has been viewed as a system, it must begin to move toward bringing about some purpose—to survive as a species, for example.

Let's look at what makes a system what it is; how those within the educational system can enhance student learning when they understand how a system works; and what people's roles are within the system. Educators have long used the term *system* when speaking of a school district or collection of schools in a community. It may seem more natural for them to understand how a system works than for others who are parts of systems that have never before been referred to in this way. Figure 2.1 demonstrates how a community of schools comprises a system, in the traditional use of the expression, *school system.* Although they

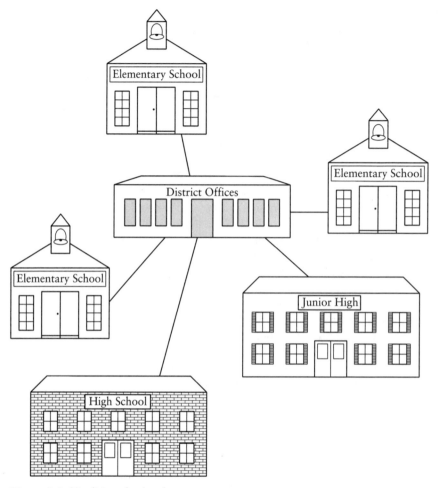

Figure 2.1: Traditional school system.

are related through the administrative function of the central offices, the buildings in a school system can often seem to be only vaguely connected with one another.

Rather than representing a series of loosely aligned buildings or units with students at different levels of schooling (as in Figure 2.1), systems have identifiable suppliers, customers, inputs and outputs, and a series of processes designed to create these outputs. Customers include those who benefit from the system and its processes and those who receive its output. These may include universities, communities, students, teachers, parents and grandparents, employers, taxing agencies, and others. Inputs to the system may include materials and techniques, environment, equipment, and people—whatever brings resources to the system so that it can produce outputs that support its purpose. These contribute to various processes that enhance the system's ability to carry out its designated purpose. It is the purpose, however, that drives the process. That is, regardless of how complicated the processes within a system may be, they are held together by a sense of their purpose and an understanding of their customers. Without that sense of driving purpose, the processes may have meanings of their own, but their contribution to the system is unclear or nonexistent.

Of course, few school systems operate without some kind of philosophy statement that articulates the values and objectives of the district. These statements, however, rarely capture the sense of purpose of the schools, and are frequently written only to satisfy regulations or to provide a lofty expression to articulate in public relations documents. Purposes that are unexpressed—such as passing on a culture to a new generation—may, in fact, be among the most important.

Systems have purpose

Systems themselves, then, are purposive. Systems such as schools are often complex and pluralistic, and they may have more than one purpose. Each system defines its own purpose, through processes of consensus, discussion, and feedback from customers both internal and external to the system. In the interest of understanding the nature of systems, however, we may simplify that purpose: Let's say that a school's ultimate purpose is to develop self-sustaining, lifelong learners.

If this is the case, what are the inputs to the system? These include, but are not limited to, buildings, teachers, audiovisual equipment, libraries, playgrounds, students, counselling services, school buses, athletic fields, and administrative offices. The contributions to the desired output are many. An adaptation of Deming's diagram of a system demonstrates relationships among these components (see Figure 2.2). How are the ways in which each component affects the output defined?

What we see is that a system—in this case, a school system—is made up of a number of subsystems. Each of the subsystems can be defined in the same terms as the larger system: suppliers and inputs; processes; outputs organized toward a purposeful end; and, of course, customers. In examining the library subsystem, for example, the following could be identified: specific environments, equipment, techniques, and materials related to the role that the library plays in bringing about lifelong learning. The library's processes would look quite different from those of the athletic fields (see Figure 2.3).

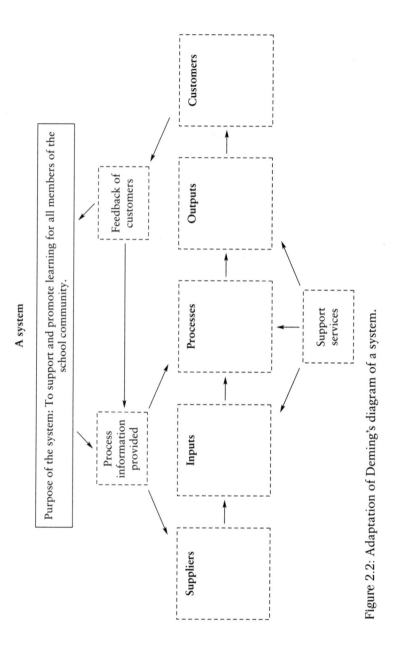

Figure 2.2: Adaptation of Deming's diagram of a system.

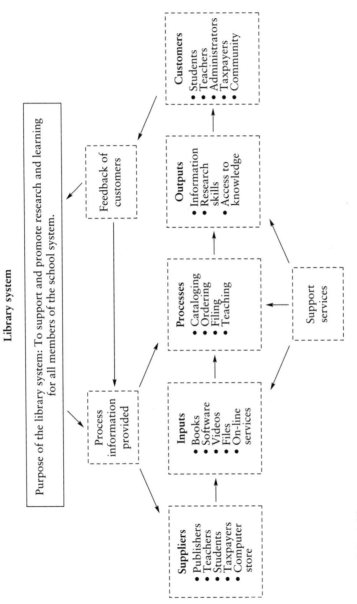

Figure 2.3: A library seen as a system.

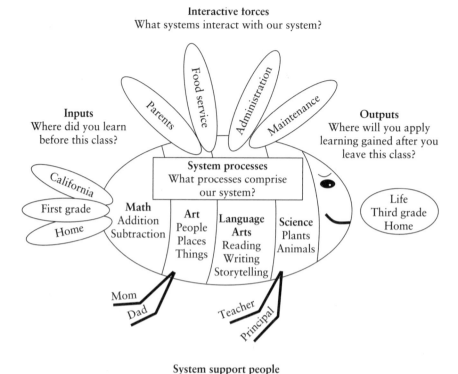

Figure 2.4: Second graders' concept of a system.

Even second graders can begin to understand the nature of a system. Figure 2.4 is a drawing of a bee that outlines the classroom system which the children experience, as this second-grade rendition demonstrates. The children who collaborated on this illustration could understand their own inputs and interaction, as well as where they expected to apply their learning after second grade. And their bee is smiling.

Subsystems and suboptimization

All processes within an organization can be considered as subsystems that must work together if the desired purpose of that organization is to be realized. This sense of unity means optimizing the system: making sure that all of its parts contribute to the success of that system in order to bring about the established purpose. Without reinforcement of this goal, the purposes of subsystems can be lost within the larger system. A library, after all, could function quite well by itself. Librarians would be hired, books ordered, resources catalogued, shelves cleaned, files organized—without a single student's ever darkening the library's doors. (In fact, from the point of view of administrative processes alone, it would be much easier that way.) What would seem to be a highly efficient, smoothly run operation would, in fact, have no purpose in the educational environment. Its processes could be flawless, but they would have no meaning. Other examples of suboptimization in a school system are readily found.

- An art history course cannot be offered because it is too hard for the principal to fit it into the schedule. (The "ideal schedule" overtakes the role that art education plays in the system's purpose.)
- A drama production is scheduled without regard to the fact that most upperclassmen will be taking advanced placement tests the same week and will be unable to participate. (Administrative tasks are simplified when students' needs can be disregarded.)
- The payroll and insurance office is always closed during the lunch hour when teachers are free to complete business-related tasks. (Business office staff members cannot do their work if their customers keep interfering.)
- Afternoon classes are cancelled so the parents' organization can prepare for a fund–raising activity. (Fund–raising has taken on a life of its own, with little connection to the learning mission of the school.)
- Parent conferences are scheduled during the day when most parents work. (Parents' needs are subverted to teacher contract stipulations.)
- An expensive but excellent calculus textbook cannot be used because the budget places an arbitrary ceiling on book prices. (The budget does not support the learning goals of the organization.)
- A classroom teacher finds herself teaching simultaneously from two different editions of a paperback novel because of the bookstore's existing inventory. (Financial pressures undermine best teaching practices.)
- A string quartet practices in a custodian's closet because the stage must be kept clean. (The custodian's needs seem to be more important than those of the music program.)
- The only ones with keys to the building are custodians. (The cus-

todial role apparently supersedes that of the knowledge staff, at least with respect to having access to the learning space in the school.)

In each case, there may appear to be a sound reason for the inconvenience or difficult situation. But these reasons are often merely excuses not to tamper with a way of doing things that is arbitrary or based on tradition. Often, the needs of individual components of the system compete with those of other components. Nowhere is this more clear than in the budgeting process. If the system works together, budget problems will be resolved to benefit the whole system. Individuals will give up trying to protect their own turf and work together to create the most beneficial budget that is possible. If everyone is in the same system, its members can work together to solve common problems.

A classroom, when it is not aligned with the purpose of the entire system, can appear to function just fine in isolation. For instance, a geometry teacher might demonstrate flawless student records, clean chalkboards, colorful and interesting posters, graphing calculators arranged neatly on desks, and even computers with modems to connect students with university resources. But if that teacher's students are not yet prepared to study geometry, or if they do not speak English, or if the teacher's methods are unfair and manipulative, or if any of a thousand other ways in which the class fails to participate in the learning process occurs, all the technology, good will, careful detail, and hard work in the world will render that subsystem ineffective. Ackoff (1990) provides the example of auto parts. Suppose from all the cars made in the world, the best transmission from one make, the best engine from another, the most efficient fuel system from another, and so on, were selected. Those parts, when put together into a car, would not function, in spite of their individual excellence.

At the same time, one of these subsystems can overtake the educational system, if the purpose of the entire system is forgotten. For example, in a school that prides itself on student performance on a national French exam, that language program may receive great attention and expanded resources in order to keep this record intact. Such a phenomenon occurs regularly in schools. It may apply to athletics programs, particular curricular areas, or outstanding individual teachers. It is easy to see how in this case, a kind of suboptimization occurs. Reducing the extreme to absurdity, it is readily seen that if the entire school day were devoted to preparing for a French test, students would continue to improve in their fluency (and their teacher would become increasingly famous). This would be an extreme example of suboptimization, where the purpose of the school is sacrificed to the purpose of the French testing system. But the same thing can occur in less dramatic ways when all members of a school community fail to understand that they contribute to a system with a purpose.

Interdependence, not isolation

When a system and its purpose are understood, what ensues is characterized by a great deal of interdependence among its components. As chapter 6 will demonstrate, this interdependence is essential to the operation of the system—and in the case of schools, to the success of the learning process itself. Different systems demonstrate different levels of interdependence. A bowling team might represent one extreme, where this interdependence is demonstrated by team support of individual effort. An orchestra illustrates a high level of interdependence. Here, individual performance is sometimes deemphasized or diminished in order to enhance the performance of the group. Regardless of the system, however, some level of interdependence is demanded among all the components of that system.

What creates a sense of teamwork, of interdependence, and of appropriate roles for particular components or subsystems, is the understanding of purpose shared by those in the system. Deming (1986) refers to "constancy of purpose" as essential to the improvement process. Once a sense of purpose is established and understood, an unwavering movement toward the accomplishment of that purpose will keep subsystems operating in the same direction. If the purpose of the educational system is simply to move students toward graduation by helping them to fulfill a series of requirements, subsystems can perform in nearly any way they choose, as long as they don't prevent a student from graduating. Most educators, however, prefer to see their roles in terms of much loftier purposes, such as providing students with understandings and skills, inspiring them to love learning, or preparing them for a learning life after they have graduated. When students and educators are able to agree on this purpose, they will find that it is easy to identify areas of improvement. The measure of the system ultimately lies in how well it fulfills its purpose.

Shared beliefs

When actions are based on shared beliefs, constancy of purpose can be developed. Therefore, these beliefs must be articulated and agreed on by those in the system. In the case of Mt. Edgecumbe High School in Sitka, Alaska, a statement of purpose was developed by students, teachers, administrators, and staff, working together to identify not only their purpose but also the shared beliefs upon which their actions would be based.

Our actions are based on the following beliefs.*

1. Human relations are the foundation for all quality improvement.
2. All components of our organization can be improved.
3. Removing the causes of problems in the system inevitably leads to improvement.
4. The person doing the job is the most knowledgeable about that job.
5. People want to be involved and do their jobs well.
6. Every person wants to feel like a valued contributor.
7. More can be accomplished by working together to improve the system than by working individually around the system.
8. A structured problem-solving process using statistical graphic problem-solving techniques lets you know where you are, where the variations lie, the relative importance of problems to be solved, and whether the changes made have had the desired impact.
9. Adversarial relationships are counterproductive and outmoded.
10. Every organization has undiscovered gems waiting to be developed.
11. Removing the barriers to pride of workmanship and joy of learning unlocks the true untapped potential of the organization.
12. Ongoing training, learning, and experimentation are a priority for continuous improvement.

*Used with permission of Mt. Edgecumbe High School.

Obviously, different people might have different lists of shared beliefs. Nonetheless, once they agree on the purpose of their system, the constancy that characterizes quality learning can follow. This agreement can be brought about by using brainstorming and then nominal group technique, tools that assure that everyone's voice is heard and that each person's prioritization of the list of beliefs is considered. Other problem-solving and team skills can support the process as well. Nominal group technique provides an opportunity for everyone not only to contribute to the list, but also to prioritize that list. Each person votes by ranking his or her top choices. If the group has agreed to select five items, for example, an individual will rank five items by assigning a numerical value to each. Higher-choice items receive 5s and 4s, while lower-choice categories receive 3s, 2s, or 1s. These are recorded and not simply added. An example is provided in Figure 2.5.

Leander Independent School District (LISD) in Texas developed a purpose statement: "The purpose of LISD is to educate each student to be successful in an ever-changing world." This purpose is translated into vision: "Each LISD graduate is prepared with the academic background and life skills to be a productive learner, an effective communicator, and a responsible citizen." A graduate profile expanded this vision into definitions of these terms and articulation of what a graduate can be with respect to each term. When school programs and student learning activities contribute unfailingly to the purpose of the school district, constancy of purpose ensues.

Another statement of purpose was developed with students in a technology course: "The purpose of Computers II is to optimize student

---

Upon what shared beliefs will we base our actions?

3-3-2-3-2	1.	Human relations are the foundation for improvement.
1-2-1	2.	All components of our organization can be improved.
1-2	3.	Removing problems leads to improvement.
2-3-1-3	4.	Those who do the job know it best.
2-1	5.	Working together will enhance system improvment.
3-1	6.	Statistical techniques can support system change.
2-1	7.	Ongoing training is a priority.
	8.	Classes and meetings should start on time.
1-1	9.	Adversarial relationships are counterproductive.
1	10.	Removing barriers to pride of workmanship and joy of learning will unlock potential.

Note: Item #1 receives the most votes.

Figure 2.5: Output of nominal group technique exercise.

understanding of theories, skills, and applications of technology to use now and in the future. If the skills are learned, they can be applied throughout life in a constant gain of knowledge and application. Decisions can be made more rapidly, accurately, and more enjoyably." In this example, students listed the following ideas, generating them by brainstorming.

- Make them required for life
- Help make future decisions
- Help make career decisions
- Need basic groundwork
- Know how to vote
- Know better how to buy
- Provide building block for successful future
- Help achieve life goals
- Hang tough, making right decisions more easily
- Know how to save safely

Once students have committed themselves to the same purpose in the class, their activities can be characterized by a sense of constancy to that purpose.

Above all, of course, what generates constancy of purpose is an understanding of the customer. The idea of having customers at all is, however, alien to most educators. For many teachers, customers are people who buy cars or take home paint samples. They stand in line to purchase stamps or international bank drafts. In the traditional usage, they are those willing to exchange their money for some service or product.

Old idea, new application

Just as *system* must be redefined, so too must *customer,* as will be seen in chapter 3. In terms of continuous improvement, customers—those who benefit from a process or system—may be internal or external to the organization. External customers may be direct or indirect. The concept may be seen from a variety of angles; sometimes the same group can be considered both as a customer and a product. Students, for example, receive the benefits that the system offers—perhaps learning opportunities. At the same time, the school in a certain sense produces students who have benefited from the learning processes that make up the educational system. Teachers are customers. They receive the benefit of certain processes in the school, such as business and administrative support services. But they are also suppliers in another sense, providing other customers—their colleagues at the next higher level, perhaps—with learning opportunities and support.

It is important to sort this out, particularly since understanding the concept of customer lies at the heart of the quality learning system, giving purpose to the organization itself. When a system is moving in the same direction, organized around the same purpose and providing clear benefit to its customers, it is orderly and predictable; when it is not, as Figure 2.6 suggests, it is chaotic and wasteful of its resources. This is true in any organization, whether it provides a manufactured product, a tangible service, or an environment.

The diagram of a system (Figure 2.2) provides some understanding about both suppliers and customers. A further exercise in identifying customers can be made by mapping the list of customers that educators can identify, both internal and external to the school, as will be demonstrated in the next chapter. This graphic representation helps to clarify relationships that exist among customers, and sometimes uncovers customers that had not been previously considered.

Systems theory, a fundamental underpinning of quality learning, is not new to the 1990s. In fact, it is not new to this century. Nineteenth-century American writers saw the connectedness of all things in the universe. Emerson's concept of the Oversoul conveyed the idea of the universe's reflection in each of its parts, and the connection of human nature and external nature to a larger system. Derived from centuries of philosophical foundations, the concept was also manifested in the writ-

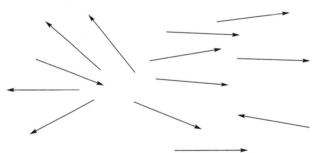

A system without a clear purpose moves in sometimes contradictory directions . . .

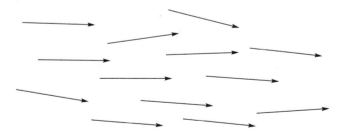

. . . unlike a system whose sense of purpose keeps it moving toward the same common aim.

Figure 2.6: System purpose.

ings of the German Idealists. Human experience resonates with the emphasis on connectedness that is currently expressed not only in the language of organizational theorists like Peter Senge, who describes the "learning organization," but also in the literature emanating from the sciences.

Moving toward systems

Once schools are seen as learning communities rather than factories, it becomes clear that they function in many of the same ways that other organizations do, and the whole world of organizational research opens to them. Systems theory pioneer Ludwig von Bertalanffry (1968), identifying the structure and function of organizations, saw systems as collections of parts with some identifiable internal relations, but with equally identifiable sets of external relationships to other systems. Certainly schools can be seen in this description, with their sense of importance to those within the system as well as their sense of accountability to the external system in which they find themselves. Interdependence among processes that make up the system is a fundamental characteristic of that system.

What we have seen is that a system is purposive—its constancy of purpose determined by an understanding of its customers. Driven by its purpose, it is made up of processes that function as subsystems to support the purpose of the larger system. Since the concept of customer represents a new way of seeing the relationship of schools to their purpose, it is important to examine this relationship in depth.

Returning to the analogy of quality learning and the elephant, we are seeing that the animal is indeed made up of parts—trunk, tail, legs, and so on—which have their own individual functions. But they are not the elephant; the animal is instead a system with a purpose (to help provide balance in the ecology of the African plain, perhaps), whose parts represent subsystems working together to make the elephant system work. Now, just who are the customers of the elephant? And where, after all, is that elephant going?

Notes

Ackoff, Russell L. 1990. *A theory of a system for educators and managers.* Produced by Clare Crawford-Mason. Written by Lloyd Dobyns. 30 min. Films, Inc. Deming Library, tape XXI.

Ackoff, Russell L., and F. E. Emery. 1972. *On purposeful systems.* Chicago: Aldine-Atherton.

Deming, W. Edwards. 1986. *Out of the crisis*. Cambridge, Mass.: MIT Center for Advanced Engineering Study.

Senge, Peter. 1990. *The fifth discipline: The art and practice of the learning organization*. New York: Doubleday.

Shah, I. 1964. *The sufis*. New York: Doubleday.

Swimme, Brian, and Thomas Berry. 1992. *The universe story*. San Francisco: HarperSan Francisco, a division of HarperCollins Publishers.

Von Bertalanffry, Ludwig. 1968. *General system theory*. New York: George Brazillier.

Chapter 3

Knowing the Customer

A system is a network of interdependent components that work together to try to accomplish the aim of the system . . . Management of a system therefore requires knowledge of the interrelationships between all the components within the system and of the people that work in it. A system must be managed. It will not manage itself. . . . The secret is cooperation between components toward the aim of the organization.

—W. Edwards Deming,
The New Economics for Business, Education, and Government

An architectural firm designing a new elementary school in Lebanon, Ohio, interviewed focus groups of the school's customers about their values in a school. Among the results were a recycling area and a comfortable place for parents to sit in the office.

Ideas like these might have been considered frills by administrators, teachers, or architectural designers, but, in fact, they reflected the community's values. By determining these values or needs and translating them into design features in the school, the architects created a building that reflected the community, developing a sense of pride and ownership along with functionality.

Two aspects of this story merit attention. First, of course, is the fact that the architects consulted the customers at all; and second, that the architects did not ask these customers what they wanted or needed. Instead, they determined values such as environmental friendliness and a welcome atmosphere for parents to visit. Then the architects used their professional expertise to translate these values into concrete features. Included in the focus groups were teachers, parents, students, custodians, staff members, and childless taxpayers.

What the architects were doing, in the language of quality, was determining customer needs, upon which they would base specific services or products. In systems talk, the architectural firm would design and develop systems to satisfy or exceed those needs. Customer expectations were also considered. Look at these dimensions of serving customers by examining another example.

Through a series of community meetings, Bergendale School District has identified a customer need to know more about what is happening in the community's schools. Members of parent organizations, service clubs, and business groups have all voiced their concerns about being kept apprised of developments in the educational system. The need is a general one, related to an area of opportunity for the school to provide information that will enhance its relationship to the community. Notice, however, that the need itself cannot be expressed in the form of a solution or specific product. When a member of the Rotary Club said, "The school needs to have a radio show," he was offering a suggestion for a solution. Underlying this assertion, however, he was expressing the same need as the parent who was complaining that the school calendar was never announced in the local newspaper. The articulations of the need were different, but the underlying need for improved communication expressed in both statements is clear.

Needs: Expressed, latent, implied

Customer needs may be expressed, latent, or implied. An expressed need is the easiest to identify. If students say, "We need to feel that our personal items will be safe in our lockers," there is little question about what their need really is.

A latent need is one that has never been expressed or even identified by customers. Latent needs are what provide opportunities for creativity and innovation, for surprising customers. In terms of products, the copy machine process can be considered a response to a latent need. That is, customers never realized that they needed this function until the copy machine became available. No one called the inventors of the copier process and asked them to develop this invention. Instead, most of us went on smearing our fingers with purple ink from an old process, without dreaming of a better way. If, after years of using copiers to satisfy their needs for duplicate print materials, schools were suddenly required to step back to duplicators such as mimeograph machines, teachers and administrators would feel that their needs were not being met. And yet, not so many years ago, they would have never articulated the copy machine among their needs. The development of the copier technology represented an active response to a latent need.

Where students and teachers bring their lunches to eat at school, latent needs might be satisfied by providing microwaves or refrigerators so that students and staff will not have to bring only the kinds of lunches that do not need to be heated or refrigerated. If a school were to provide these amenities, diners would initially be delighted by the expanded possibilities for lunch. Once changes are in place, however, they become expectations. Hot lunch programs, now standard in most public schools, were beyond imagination in early schools, although students have always needed to eat. New expectations arise because of organizations' responses to needs. Like other organizations, schools have sometimes been reluctant to raise expectations about the educational process, for fear that these expectations could not be met.

From the earliest days of formal schooling, students have had a need to get from their homes to the school. Once that need could no longer be satisfied by walking, a variety of possibilities for transportation emerged. In a New Jersey suburb, students from one town rode the train to the adjoining town so they could attend school there. Public transportation has expanded in some areas, so that students travel by subway, city bus, or trolley. In some places they travel by airplane or boat. Carpools have developed to create convenience for parents and diminish fuel costs. Ultimately, students began to drive family cars to school. A long-standing need for transportation has been satisfied in a variety of ways, including school bus systems that were developed as school districts were consolidated and traveling distances increased.

Students do not need school buses; they need transportation. But bus transportation has become an expectation in many districts. Ask parents what would happen if school buses were no longer provided to transport children to school—something that has happened in financially pressed school districts. The need for transportation has become an expectation that schools will provide such transportation by means of buses. Gone are the days when students were expected to walk several miles to school because there were no other options. The system of transportation that has been provided in response to an identified need has altered expectations among its users.

One need that students have always experienced is that of a safe environment. Parents have expected that their children's safety would not be threatened in schools. Traditionally, schools responded to that need by assuring adult supervision of students, disciplining bullies on the playground, and regularly inspecting fire emergency equipment. The need remains for students to be safe, but schools are having to respond in new and creative ways to increasing numbers and kinds of assaults on students' physical well-being. Metal detectors, trained dogs, and armed security officers appear in many school buildings. In this example, the need has not changed, but the response to that need has required change.

When needs become expectations

For many school districts, expectations have not been challenged by expanding technology, and customers find their needs satisfied in sometimes primitive ways. A new administrator of the Cincinnati public school system, given a tour of the facilities, found antiquated data-entry cards and keypunch machines—not state-of-the-art computers. He was appalled when employees proudly pointed to the keypunch machine, for he had not seen this kind of equipment in use for more than 20 years. His response was, "This is not customer-oriented—and it's got to go." (Bradley 1993)

For students who have expressed the need for a safe place for their belongings, the school might respond in a variety of ways. A traditional response is that of secure lockers for coats and books. Other approaches might be to reorganize the school so that students remain in the same rooms throughout the day (with their possessions), and teachers come in to instruct the students. Security police might guard an area where students keep their things. Electronic surveillance equipment might allow students and teachers to know what is happening in the student commons. Students might have assigned wagons, to cart their things with them. A checkroom might even be provided for safe storage, or storage cubbies could be built in every classroom.

An implied need, unlike an expressed need, is one that is not articulated because it is so fundamental to the customer's understanding of the need itself. If teachers were asked to develop a list of needs for a new computer facility, a great deal of attention would go into various aspects of the program design. The final list might include the need for flexibility in space and scheduling, the opportunity for several students to be instructed simultaneously, and the ability to provide adequate storage for support materials. Almost certainly, it would not even occur to the teachers to express a need to install electricity in the building so the computers could be operated. That need is so fundamental to the operation of the facility that it is not even necessary to express it. If, however, the designer responded to every one of the teachers' expressed needs but failed to install electricity, the teachers would be outraged and incredulous.

Implied needs—because they have become givens—are what prevent customer dissatisfaction rather than creating satisfaction. Ordering a customized burger, a diner might request tomatoes, a whole wheat bun, lettuce, and pickles. If the burger were served raw, the customer would be outraged. While the chef might legitimately respond, "You didn't mention that you wanted me to cook the meat," cooking the meat is such a fundamental part of the customer's implied needs that it should not have to be mentioned. Parents may express the need for school bus schedules that provide for timely arrivals at school. They should not have to express the need for drivers to obey the speed limit, or to stop the school bus to pick up children along the route. (Yet, drivers could, in fact, arrive at school in a consistently prompt and timely way by driving too fast and by not picking up any students.)

An implied student need might be to be able to enter the building during class time so that the learning process can take place within the system provided. Imagine classrooms that are well equipped with adequate lighting, sufficient textbooks, maps, desks, and other accoutrements that support learning, but that are kept locked so students cannot enter them for class. It goes without saying that teachers, students, parents, and taxpayers would be incredulous. Yet it is unlikely that this basic need would be listed by customers of the system. It is a given. What might seem to be a given, however, is sometimes not considered to be an implied need. In most companies, for example, employees can have access to their offices on weekends or evenings, either through a security system or by having their own keys to the facilities. Schools rarely provide this kind of access to teachers. In many districts it is unlikely that teachers will have keys even to their own classrooms or work areas.

To respond to the community's need for enhanced communication, school administrators might brainstorm a variety of possibilities, including a radio show, a column in the local newspaper, or a newsletter to parents. The need does not demand only one response. Customer satisfaction derives from an appropriate response to the need, even if it is one that customers had not anticipated.

Identifying the customer

Determining customer needs and expectations is critical to designing systems that will meet these needs and expectations. But none of this can happen without actually identifying who the customer is—a step often overlooked when organizations operate on assumptions about whom they serve rather than gathering data to create information.

Customers are those who receive any of the benefits provided by a system. In the food service system, for example, it might be obvious that the customers are those who consume the food that is provided. What is less obvious, however, is that for each of the subsystems within the larger system, customers can be identified. Systems have both internal and external customers. If George is a food server in the school cafeteria, he is a customer of his colleague who has handed him a plate to be filled for George's customer—the student waiting for hot food. Everyone in the system can be seen both as a customer and as a supplier, just as this food server is. With respect to identifying needs and expectations, there is little difference between these two types of customers; but in determining all customers of the system, it is important to remember that there are both internal and external customers.

Customers who are external to a system may be either direct—those who immediately benefit from the services or products of the system; or indirect—customers who have significant interest in the system but are neither internal to it nor directly receive its benefits. An example of an indirect customer in a school system might be a state agency. An accrediting agency, for example, receives various written reports and observations from the school district. Its need is to learn as much as it can about the school district. When the agency approves the accreditation, it becomes a supplier, supporting the school district's need to know how it compares to other schools in the state. The agency has had the benefit of the school's willingness to share information about its programs, but does not share directly in the fundamental services and products that the school provides.

A critical question, then, is who receives the services of the schools? One first response might be, its students. Certainly, students are direct beneficiaries of many of the school's services. Seen in another way, however, if the school's purpose is to produce well-educated students with skills and knowledge to contribute to society, it is society itself that receives the direct benefit of this product. Some would identify parents as the direct customers of the system. Remember, however, that the system—seen as an entire system—does not, in fact, prepare students to live with their parents for life. One might also see the university system or prospective employers as direct customers of the system.

Classifying customers is useful because it causes us to think about the relationships among all those who are customers of the system. The classification itself, however, is less important than this process. Another observation is that the process of identifying customers is directly related to the understanding of purpose in a system.

In the interest of focusing on customers, it is useful to begin with a list. If the question were to identify all those who receive the products and services of the school system itself as well as its subsystems, we would again see that customers are often suppliers as well. When a teacher prepares students for the next-level teaching process, that teacher is a supplier to the next; the second teacher, in turn, becomes a supplier to the next-advanced process, and so on.

A customer list generated in a school system might look like the following:

- Society
- Colleges and universities
- Teachers
- Special-education teachers
- Counsellors
- Employers
- The environment
- Administrators
- Psychologists
- Other support staff

- Board of education
- Vendors
- Political systems
- Students
- Funding sources
- State agencies
- Contractors
- Families
- Economic systems
- Taxpayers
- Future generations

All of these components have needs related to the school system. A quality learning organization creates systems to respond to as many of these needs as possible. But needs themselves cannot be measured. Even when a need is explicitly stated—the students' expressed need for a feeling that their belongings are safe, for example—one can only guess when that need is really satisfied. Methods to communicate customer needs to the system are seriously lacking in current school systems.

How then do the managers of a system know when customer needs have been satisfied, or how to improve customer satisfaction? Something has to be measurable in order to be improved in measurable ways. (Teachers can improve their relationship with students, but teachers will not be able to measure that improvement.)

Organizations respond to the needs of their customers with specific products and services. On the basis of these responses, customers develop expectations. Most students expect to enter a high school building and find lockers where they can store their personal belongings. Their need (unmeasurable) is satisfied when the school administrators make lockers available. Expectations related to that service can indeed be measured. Students will expect lockers to be secure, easy to open, clean (in the beginning, at least), and functional. Each of these expectations can be seen in terms of quality measures. Data can be collected to demonstrate how many locker doors stick, for example. Improvement measures are based on data related to expectations. A maintenance team can repair all the locks so they work smoothly even before students complain about them. If the team has identified the customer need—security for belongings—and established quality measures related to expectations—ability to lock the door easily, for example—it can continue to meet students' needs and ultimately exceed them.

Customers of internal systems

Customers' needs, then, are satisfied by specific products or services that are offered by a system. Examine customers of a subsystem within the schools—say, the system of teaching mathematics. The list might include all the math teachers from primary through high school grades, the computer center, current and future employers of students, universities, students, and parents. Examining the mathematics function in more specific terms, a smaller subsystem might be a single classroom where advanced algebra is taught. This subsystem has customers too.

For example, who are the customers of Ms. Ferraro's fifth-period precalculus class, and what are their needs and expectations? The list might include the following:

- Mr. Wilson, calculus teacher, who will teach these students next year
  —He *needs* to have students ready to learn in his classroom.
  —He *expects* that after being in Ms. Ferraro's class, students will have competence with skills necessary for higher study.
- Physics, chemistry, and computer teachers
  —They *need* students who are able to expand and apply mathematical concepts.
  —They *expect* basic preparation and an understanding of specific applications.
- Mr. Lofino, who employs students part time in his grocery store
  —He *needs* employees who can serve his customers well.
  —He *expects* that they can calculate and make change.
- The bank where students keep the money they have earned at Mr. Lofino's store
  —The bank *needs* customers who will continue to save and invest.
  —The bank *expects* all customers to understand basic financial and mathematical principles.
- Local retailers
  —They *need* assurance that they will have customers for their goods.
  —They *expect* customers to have problem-solving and decision-making skills that will lead them to make appropriate purchases.
- Ms. Fuller, coach of the math team that competes in local contests
  —She *needs* students who love math.
  —She *expects* her team to demonstrate its math performance.
- Parents of students in Ms. Ferraro's class
  —They *need* to know that their sons and daughters are learning.
  —They *expect* frequent reports about students' educational progress.
- Taxpayers
  —They *need* to have value for their investment.
  —They *expect* demonstration of math skills.

- Society
  —It *requires* contributions that will assure the future of civilization.
  —It *expects* critical thinking skills that will give leadership to the community.
- Students themselves
  —They *need* to develop confidence in their understanding of the concepts, skills, and applications of mathematics.
  —They *expect* to be able to apply their learning to new situations and problems.

In this example, we can see that while the *needs* of each customer group are not clearly measurable, their *expectations* about the specific product or service—in this case, the precalculus course—can be easily observed, measured, and evaluated. It is on the basis of those expectations that quality learning can improve the educational process.

Responding to needs: A moving target

The response to students' need to learn math lies in a specific classroom experience. The response to students' need for preparation so they will be able to perform at the next stage, whether it is in the workplace where they share the benefits of their educations with employers, or the next phase of their formal education where they demonstrate their readiness for higher thinking or enhanced skill acquisition, is developed by the school system. Expectations about the school system belong to all of its customers. Some of these expectations are similar, and others are quite diverse, creating a tapestry of expectations woven from addressing customer needs.

Specific preparation for life work is sometimes an expectation that students and their parents have of the school system. ("All that education and couldn't even get a job.") When graduates are unable to get jobs or to succeed in them, they sometimes feel that school has failed them. If specific preparation for a particular occupation is their goal, students will undoubtedly be disappointed in their educations. But how many adults are actually working in the skill areas for which they prepared? And, of these, how many are utilizing the same understandings that they had when they began? Those who began their work prior to technological changes, for example, were in one sense totally unprepared for job life. Preparation for an occupation is a need, and can be anticipated in a larger context than that of specific job skills.

Those who know how to learn and how to work well with others will succeed in their positions regardless of how many times the work life changes. Sadly, many of those now unemployed may have been well equipped with a specific set of skills and aptitudes, but not with the larger understandings that they would need for lifetime success in their working lives. Employers, as customers of the school system, can help students understand the knowledge that they will need to assure this success. Willis Harman (1988) suggests that the promotion of lifelong learning becomes a "central project" of any society that does not have to utilize a large percentage of its resources to simply survive.

In this, as in every other system, customers' needs as well as their expectations are dynamic. They will change on the basis of how their needs have been met (or not met) in the past. In examining the math list, for example, it may be surprising to note that most local retailers do not really expect their customers to have these skills. In fact, unscrupulous store owners may hope that customers are not equipped to buy wisely, so that they will buy junk, and create unethical profits for the owners. Employers, sadly enough, have diminished expectations of the abilities of graduates to perform, and have spent millions of dollars to overcome employees' inability to demonstrate competence with basic skills. The public's expectations of schools, tempered by their past failure to provide well-educated students, are discouraging.

If these expectations are based on past experiences, then the connection between the system and customer expectations is clear. But, fundamentally, customer needs must be identified if these expectations are to improve. There are ways to monitor customer needs in consistent ways. Leander Independent School District in Texas has established a "transition coordinator" to help students understand alternative possibilities for them after high school. "We devote 13 intense years to students, and then say 'good luck' and 'good-bye' the minute they have walked across the stage at graduation," an administrator points out—explaining the need to bridge the transition between one kind of customer need (that of students) and another (that of graduates). In the same way, some independent schools have developed systems to monitor graduates' adjustment to college, in order to determine how well prepared they were for what lay ahead.

Needs and accountability

One dramatic response to concerns about the educational system has been an insistence on accountability by means of mandated testing—a demand that has taken hold across the United States. Taxpayers and other external customers, requiring knowledge of how well schools are preparing students, have latched on to a system of standardized testing in order to capture this knowledge.

Testing represents a flawed attempt to measure how well customers' expectations for competent graduates are being met by the system that is in place to satisfy their needs. Seen only in terms of our discussion of customer needs and expectations, testing cannot measure customer needs, since these are not measurable. This is an important distinction to make here, since, as we have seen, expectations are based on the performance of the system. Depending on how they are used, standardized tests can represent a response only to negative expectations, rather than a way to evaluate how well the ultimate needs of the system's customers are being met. To pursue this idea further, examine the role of standardized testing with respect to satisfying the following needs.

- Students' need to learn
- Teachers' need to support learning
- Taxpayers' need for value
- Society's need for competent citizens

Of this group, student and teacher needs are related most directly to the learning process itself. For these customers, testing can be a helpful tool in evaluating areas of competence and assure mastery of concepts. A test can help students answer the question, "How well do I know this?" The best test helps students to apply a concept or to solve a problem, so that they can collaborate with their teacher in determining where further attention to the learning process is required. A teacher tests students every day, usually in informal ways. "Karla, how can we find out whether this is a sonnet or not?" is a discussion question that will elicit information to help the teacher and students evaluate progress and to plan for future growth. Even a multiple-choice test, if students are asked to evaluate, as Deming suggests, the circumstances under which each possible answer might be correct, can reflect this kind of feedback. In an informal way, students can evaluate their own levels of competence with a particular skill by means of an informal *consensogram,* which suggests how much more attention needs to be given to developing that skill (see Figure 3.1). Students may be asked to assess their own level of competence with a particular skill, or their understanding of a concept. When students are challenged to evaluate whether they are 100 percent confident of interviewing skills, for example, they are participating in the learning process and giving direction to how further needs will be addressed.

A state-mandated standardized test, on the other hand, does not offer this opportunity. It is an end-of-the-process instrument designed to measure acquisition of certain skills and to be used as an instrument of evaluation of the school. This standardized test is not useful to individual students, since it does not give them information that will help to de-

How confident are you of your interviewing skills?

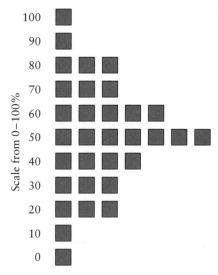

Figure 3.1: Langford consensogram.

termine their next step in learning. It is not useful to teachers except in negative ways: This group of students has failed.

To taxpayers or employers, and indeed to society itself, the test instrument seems to be a way to measure the schools' ability to meet large needs. The process of standardized tests, however, is based on an expectation that the schools themselves and the internal customers of the system (teachers, students) cannot really evaluate progress and improve the system themselves. The expectation of failure, rather than one of success, is what has brought about the current cry for standardized test scores. Standardized testing does not respond to fundamental needs of the internal customers of the system for improvement and enhancement of the learning process. Furthermore, interpretation of test results is often not framed in a solid understanding of variability, as will be seen in chapter 4. An understanding of variation and a genuine desire to use testing for improvement could result in tests that are given anonymously to a random sampling of students, to provide managers of the system with indicators of how well the system is performing with respect to specific measures. The only "use" that can be seen for massive and expensive testing programs is that of marketing; and rather than focusing on ways to improve the learning system itself, convincing external customers that everything inside is okay. Chapter 5 will return to this idea.

As Lloyd Dobyns rightly observes, however, such testing "is nothing more than a final inspection and won't make the kid coming out of

school (or the car coming off the assembly line) a damned bit better."
He adds that any competent teacher can tell how well a student per-
forms, long before any final test is administered.

Customer needs, variation, and improvement

On the other hand, supported by an understanding of variation and a
commitment to improvement, test results could provide valuable information about how well the system is doing. A control chart could reflect
the stability of the system in producing desired learning outcomes.
Quality learning, with its emphasis on creating systems to identify and
serve the needs of customers and understanding variability within the
system, gives the responsibility for improvement of the system back to
the system owners—students, teachers, and administrators—rather than
depending on external, artificial measures of success and failure. In this
scenario, test results help owners understand their system and predict its
performance in the long run.

It is the nature of customer needs and expectations that they are
built on prior experiences with the system that is in place. If that system
were to be improved, expectations would simultaneously improve.
Using quality learning concepts, schools can bring genuine improvement
to the system of learning. And if the learning process is improved, the
expectations of all those served by the schools will be enhanced, creating a cycle of continuous improvement based on expectations of success
rather than predictions of failure.

When standardized tests are administered as a way to assure accountability, such tests fail to understand one of the fundamental characteristics shared by all systems. This characteristic is variation, which
deserves a close look in the next chapter.

Notes

Bradley, Ann. 1993. The business of reforming Cincinnati's schools. *Education
Week*, 19 May, 1.

Deming, W. Edwards. 1993. *The new economics for business, education, and
government*. Cambridge, Mass.: MIT Center for Advanced Engineering
Study.

Dobyns, Lloyd. 1994. Correspondence with authors, 15 May.

Harman, Willis. 1988. *Global mind change*. Indianapolis: Knowledge Systems.

Chapter 4

Understanding Variation

Such a life, with all vision limited to a Point, and all motion to a Straight Line, seemed to me inexpressibly dreary.

—Edwin A. Abbott,
Flatland

It's time to stop reading and try something. Instead of continuing to read, go back and count the number of times the letter *A* appears in the final two paragraphs of chapter 3. An operational definition of *A* is, "the first letter of the alphabet, either uppercase or lowercase, as it appears either within a word or by itself as an article, any time within the two defined paragraphs."

Record your count. Now count the *A*s again.

Was your second count the same as your first? If there had been a time limit, or you were not allowed to point with your finger or your pencil, would your count have been the same?

If your count was the same each time you checked the two paragraphs, no variation occurred. If 25 people counted the number of *A*s, their answers would probably not represent 25 different answers, but they would undoubtedly not all be the same; there would be some variation among the counts. (There is a correct answer—50—but not everyone would necessarily see all the *A*s on the first try.)

Fundamental to quality learning is an understanding of the statistical concept of variation and the ability to know when a process has actually changed. If you counted the *A*s by using a pencil to cross each one off as it was counted, the process would be a little different from one in which you are expected to read the paragraphs as they are projected on a screen at the front of a classroom. Or if you did not have an operational definition that included both uppercase and lowercase letters and you were counting only lowercase *A*s, your outcome would have been different. If you included the endnotes in what you counted, you would have found more *A*s. In terms of understanding processes, comprehending the significance of variation puts an organization's improvement energy where it belongs rather than responding willy-nilly to every trivial change. It helps to address the problems that matter and to improve the areas that can be improved.

Variation is everywhere

Every process has variation. Even an excellent student will not score exactly the same on all measurement evaluations such as tests. An excellent English student will experience ups and downs in the writing process, with some papers turning out better—that is, offering fewer opportunities for improvement—than others. If the same group of students were to be given the same standardized test every single week, there would be variation in the results. A good speller may spell the same word differently within the same paper or during different weeks.

We might expect that test scores would improve each time a group is retested; and this might indeed be the case, even if the questions were changed, given enough review of the concepts being tested. But if that logic were followed to its extreme, we could expect not only that, eventually, every student would answer every question right, but also that on each sequential test, all scores would improve at some incremental rate. Natural variation in the process precludes this outcome. Even students who know material well are subject to distraction, carelessness, memory lapse, tension, illness, and a variety of other factors that may influence the outcome of a single test. Natural variation will always be a part of the process, even when it is controlled by repetitive testing. Certainly, variation will occur when no such control is exerted.

This variation or difference is a fundamental concept for the study of any process, whether tangible or intangible. A simple numerical example occurs in every classroom of students. When teachers walk into a classroom for the first time, they can immediately identify some degree of variation among the students. Teachers may distinguish different heights, for example, among the group members. This is simple variation.

Collecting data and charting the data points helps to understand the variation in heights. Suppose someone were to compile height data in this classroom. Using inches to represent height and rounding up to the nearest inch, the following numbers might be recorded.

42 44 48 54 50 46 46 50 50 48 52 56 48 44 52 48 58

As in the case of the sports broadcaster who announces, "And now for the scores: 4, 0, 7, 12, 3, 6, 26, and 14," this list of numbers in itself has no meaning. Additional analysis is necessary. The numbers could be ranked from low to high or high to low, and this would give a better sense of the range of the heights. The *histogram,* or bar chart, is a tool that presents data graphically in terms of the number of occurrences. This tool can be helpful in analyzing these numbers, because it clearly identifies the number of times a specific height occurs. In the histogram in Figure 4.1, the variation among the heights can be seen as the numbers are examined. In fact, after calculating the average height—49.17"—it may be that no single student is actually that height. The histogram thus helps to understand variation among the heights, rather than to focus on the individuals and their specific heights.

Understanding the paradigm of quality learning forces people to take a close look at what once seemed obvious. While height differences among 17 students may not seem to be earth-shattering information in itself, the example is important in developing an understanding of variation. Unless there were a special reason to create similarity among the students, such as a selection process to assure that every student in the class were at least five feet tall, we would never expect to find a standardized height among a group of students in the classroom. We accept this kind of variation, just as we accept variation in the way popcorn pops—we do not expect every kernel to pop at the same time or in the

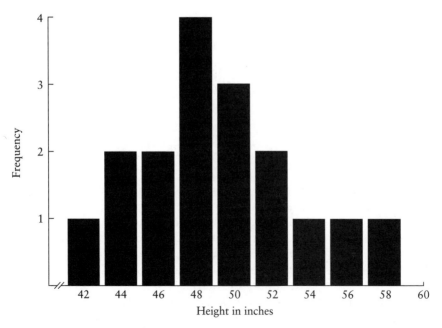

Figure 4.1: Histogram of heights.

same shape. A problem is not perceived just because not every student is among the tallest.

Collecting data

Examining variation in every aspect of the educational system reveals patterns, problems, and trends. Collecting data over time suggests these patterns. If we were to focus on height at a given moment as a reflection of some kind of achievement level, half of our students would be below average. But for the most part, we accept this variation not as success or failure, but simply as variation. Height, of course, has little to do with the educational process. This same kind of natural variation will exist in every process in the organization. For example, does the same percentage of students score above 1400 on the Scholastic Aptitude Test (SAT) every year? Do all book orders placed on the same day arrive at the same time? Do all students suddenly, at the same moment, master the fundamentals of irregular Spanish verbs or multiplication tables? Do all teachers dismiss their classes at the exact same instant? Will a school bus arrive at a given stop at the same moment every day? The answer to all of these questions is, no, of course not. Is this a problem? Sometimes it is, sometimes it is not. The key to improvement lies in understanding the natural variation that already exists with processes, identifying the causes for variation, and then developing a theory to reduce that variation so that the entire system can be improved. Reacting when there is no reason to act, or failing to react when there is, both reflect limited understanding of variation. Interpreting outcomes is likely to be faulty without this understanding, as Deming points out, for an explanation of every event is then often sought in terms of some person or some other event to blame. In fact, Deming (1986) asserts that more than 85 percent of the causes of variation lie in the system.

The same variation applies to the learning process. At a given moment in time, half of the students in a group will fall below the average of the group with respect to their acquisition of a particular skill or understanding. At age one, children are at various stages of learning to walk. Although proud parents like to link early walking with precocity, statistics suggest a wide range of ages when children take their first steps, all of which are considered quite normal. Acquiring conversational proficiency with Spanish verbs will reflect the same kinds of variation. Some students may need more time, different kinds of reinforcement, a variety of learning techniques, and so on, to master these verbs. Interpreting the outcome of one test, based on a single classroom style, as an indicator of what a student knows does a great disservice to that student. Learning is not binomial ("I know something or I don't"); rather, it is accrued ("I know a little more about exponents today than I did yesterday"). Students in any group will have arrived at different levels of mastery.

Children's weight gains reflect variability, as do the amounts of hair they may have on their heads. If we were to set in motion a set of evaluations of these patterns, or a standard achievement level, many children would be failures by the age of two. It strikes us as ludicrous to think of counselling a child to try to be as tall as his classmates, or to assign him a grade of C in height; and yet we may use these techniques when it comes to other developmental patterns, such as reading readiness or abstract thinking skills. Understanding variation will help us to identify the times when that variation must be addressed by changing something in the system and when this variation is a part of the natural growth process. Statistically speaking, *below the average* is not a pejorative term.

To analyze trends and to address problems, it is essential to track data over time, rather than relying on a single moment of measurement or observation. Since things either stay the same or are increasing or decreasing, what is important is not what is happening only today. Using the height variation data, it would not be alarming to find that an eight-year-old student is 38" tall on a particular date. If, however, over time that child's height never changes, falling further and further below the average height for his or her age, additional analysis would be in order. When a student learns new material and is tested on it, the results may show a lack of mastery of the material; they also indicate that more (or different) learning opportunities will be required. A single data point cannot be considered the final measure of a process. *Point thinking* occurs when people mistake that single data point for a trend.

Trends and not-yet trends

Interpreting data with respect to variation demands recognition of the causes for that variation. In the example of SAT scores, school districts often publicize their numbers of National Merit finalists to demonstrate the prowess of the district itself, even comparing their numbers to those of other districts. The chances are if scores are collected over a long period—25 years or more—the variations that occur in an individual district's scores will be predictable and stable. If a district's average scores over time are generally high, this may be due to a number of factors, including the demographics of the community, rather than to the excellence of the learning process. Likewise, a pattern of lower scores may reflect a community's makeup, the educational and economic levels of parents, and other factors. In both cases, the scores are likely to remain within a predictable level of variation, unless something special occurs to alter the pattern. (If the district receives another district's test scores by mistake, for example, that would represent a dramatic cause for variation in the data. Or if all students had been coming down with chicken pox when they took the test.)

When data points are charted over time, it becomes clear when a trend emerges. Look at another sample of data. If student attendance at optional study sessions were monitored, would the following decline seem to be significant?

> October 20: 89 percent attended
> December 18: 64 percent attended
> January 14: 61 percent attended
> February 18: 47 percent attended

With only these data points to consider, it might be alarming to find what seems to be a steady decline in attendance. After all, the percentage attending the sessions seems to have dropped steadily from a high of 89 percent to a mere 47 percent. Without the proper tools of analysis, the numbers are subject to interpretation, opinion, and misunderstanding. Look at the data charted over a longer period of time, since four data points, selected at random over a period of several months, are too few to make accurate observations about the process. By using a *run chart* and plotting data in a uniform way over enough actual time, it is possible to begin to understand the implications of the data even with no further analysis. A run chart offers a way to record data points chronologically. In this case, what emerges with clarity is the fact that what seemed to be a dramatic decline is part of a regular pattern of ups and downs in attendance at the study sessions (see Figure 4.2).

Other steps can be taken with this chart to determine if the process that it describes is stable; that is, whether the ups and downs in the data are within the expectations of normal variability, or whether the process is out of control, with erratic fluctuations that indicate that its direction is not predictable. If the variation in a process falls between statistically calculated control limits, it is said to be "stable." If not, it is out of control. (A simple formula for calculating these limits is provided in the glossary.) *Control charts* help to identify the stability of the system, pointing the way for improvement of that system. While they may be produced on computer programs or recorded on sophisticated, preprinted charting paper, control charts may also be created by hand. French teacher Claire Curtice, for example, produced such a chart on graph paper for her French II students' performance levels. The important aspect of creating control charts is the interpretation; a teacher can stimulate questions about the data when she shows it to students, as Curtice did in her French class. Among the questions she asked were the follow-

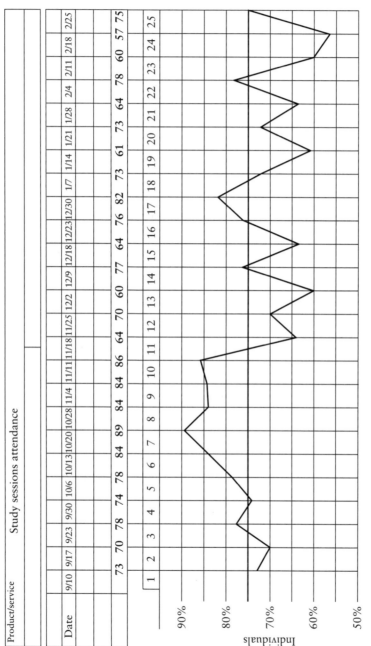

Figure 4.2: Run chart for study session attendance.

ing: "Does this reflect your best effort? What class average do we want on the next test? How did you study? What could I, as your teacher, do better? What percent effort does this test represent for you? What specific things can you do to improve the class average?" (A French teacher takes on control charts 1993).

When to react to changes

Even before calculating control limits, the first step in data analysis is to look at the story that the chart tells. What is immediately apparent, for example, is that no conclusions can be made based on only four arbitrarily selected data points previously presented. Once we have examined these data points as they relate to consistently charted data over a period of time, we see that using them involves taking them out of context and acting as if they represent a trend. Even if the four points were consecutive (as are the three downward points on February 4, 11, and 18), they would not present any clear picture about the situation. Far more data must be collected. At least 25 data points are recommended for sound analysis.

All measurements will have their natural ups and downs, whether they relate to attendance or student performance. If efforts to improve were made every time a measurement point declines, an organization would be spending all of its time reacting to such shifts. The point is to react when it is important to react, not every time something seems different. If a student has a perfect attendance record and is absent for four days straight, the absences need to be considered in terms of the larger pattern rather than in isolation. Is that student's record, for example, different from that of another student who is absent for four days in a row, but who has frequently been absent for longer periods? Of course it is. The second student's attendance pattern might require action with respect to determining cause, while the first student—perhaps sick for the first time in his or her life—requires something quite different from the school upon returning.

The key to improving processes lies in understanding what is natural variation created by causes that occur throughout the data points (*common causes*), and what can be identified as particular circumstances (*special causes*) that create data points outside the control limits. In the study session example, every individual date is subject to some of the same situations. Students may have outside jobs; they sometimes go out of town with their families; and their work loads vary from day to day and week to week. These are common causes of variation. It would be unrealistic to expect that the same number of students would attend these sessions every day.

Someone who is familiar with the process, who is well acquainted with these study sessions, knows most about these variations and what causes them. The common causes for student absences contribute to the variation that falls within control limits that have been calculated. These causes include personal illness or injury, family crisis, travel, and so on. When a point lies outside these control limits, however, special causes of variation—those that are not ordinarily part of the entire system—must be sought.

On February 18, for example, it might be determined that there had been a flu outbreak after the Valentine's Day dance, and that attendance at school as well as all extracurricular events had declined. This was not a regular and frequently recurring problem, but one that had a very specific origin—a special cause. There is no need to change the entire system of study sessions to respond to this cause on a long-term basis.

To analyze the data further, control limits are calculated and an assessment made about the stability of the entire system; that is, whether it falls within predictable limits. Even before pursuing this statistical calculation, the data points indicate something about the process; with further analysis, even more is revealed about that process.

So what? Dealing with variation

Once a system is determined to be stable, work on improving the system as a whole can begin. The greatest effort will not be put into responding to individual decreases, such as that which occurred after the Valentine's Day dance, but instead will focus on the larger issue of helping students take advantage of the resources available. The purpose of the study sessions is to help students. If these sessions are not useful or are scheduled at inconvenient times such as when students are likely to be off campus, the data will indicate whether students are utilizing these helpful sessions. The data will perhaps raise the question, how can these sessions be more useful, rather than the issue, how can we force those who don't attend to be there, or how can we improve attendance.

Examples of this kind of analysis of variation can be found throughout the school system. If a bus arrives at its stop day after day within a 5-minute period of time, the process of getting the bus to its stop is undoubtedly a stable one. If it varies by 20 minutes or more on a single day, that delay may be due to a special cause such as icy road conditions. It is undesirable to change the entire process of bus scheduling on the basis of that single data point. On the other hand, if the bus were to arrive 20 minutes late—or 20 minutes early—every day for an extended period of time (a run of 7 instances or more), the process should be closely examined. By collecting a sufficient amount of data and analyzing the stability of the system, we can predict with some accuracy how that system will operate in the future. Without the occurrence of a special cause (such as an ice storm, for example), the bus route will probably arrive at school at about the same time each morning. *About the same time* means that its arrival will fall within statistically calculated control limits.

In another example, we all know what happens when classroom thermostats are adjusted throughout a day with every judgment of temperature change. The first class of the day feels a chill, and the heat is turned up; the second-period class arrives, finds the room hot and stuffy, turns down the thermostat, and opens the windows. Students in the next class announce that they are "freezing," and the pattern goes on throughout the day. Reacting to every change by readjusting the thermostat results in wasted energy, inconsistently uncomfortable teaching environments, and attention diverted unproductively from the day's study of *The Scarlet Letter.* This kind of tampering with the system is a natural reaction when variation is not understood and addressed as part of that system and when analysis is not based on data collected over time.

Using the system of quality learning, data would be collected over a significant period of time—perhaps by measuring the temperature in the room at the beginning of all class periods over a two-week period. That data could then be charted and analyzed for what is revealed about the variation in classroom temperatures. An improvement theory could then be developed by reacting to the data rather than reacting to each individual fluctuation. Ultimately, it may be that the thermostat is set too low in the morning, and that if it is raised a degree or two before classes begin, the room would remain comfortable all day. It is essential to gather and analyze the data in a process rather than merely speculating on what might work to improve the system. Using a similar problem, a Junior Achievement class in a high school in Middletown, Ohio, undertook a study of temperature control in the building after noticing a great deal of variation in the comfort level among classrooms. Team members gathered data from several rooms (on both sunny and shady sides of the building), charted their findings, developed a theory about improvement and tested it, then made a recommendation to a group made up of the principal, the head of maintenance, several teachers, and the students' advisor. Action was ultimately taken to decrease the variability and render the rooms uniformly comfortable.

Understanding variation and improving the classroom

Within an individual classroom, a teacher can also understand a process by looking at its variation. If a history teacher perceives that participation in class discussions seems to be dwindling, for example, he might be tempted to threaten his students (usually with grades), lecture them about the benefits of participation, or in some other way shift the problem to students. If these discussions do not improve, he will perhaps become more adamant, and his relationship with his class will hold even less promise for cooperative improvement efforts. If, on the other hand, the teacher were to collect data about the number of students who actually participate, he would be better prepared to formulate a theory for improvement. By identifying the variation he will know if the system is stable and could therefore be improved as a system, or if there are particular special causes for that variation—such as high absenteeism on a given day. He and his students can examine the data together and pursue the improvement process. Then, not only is classroom participation likely to improve, but also students' awareness of and sense of responsibility for their own learning are enhanced.

The process, as charted by a teacher over a period of several weeks, is reflected in Figure 4.3, where data points have been recorded in the standard run chart format used to monitor processes, whether they are related to manufacturing or service delivery systems. A control chart is made from the same data after calculating the average and the ranges among the data points (see Figure 4.4). It is readily seen that the variation that occurs falls within predictable ranges. Thus the system can be said to be stable. Even though this is the case, however, it may be that it is not at the level that both the teacher and his students might desire. Therefore, they can proceed to develop theories about how to improve the entire system of classroom discussion, implement and test those theories, and then standardize the improvements that have worked.

In the school system, an understanding of variation can help students, teachers, administrators, and parents to improve a number of situations. First, it helps them to understand the situation: whether something represents normally recurring circumstances or whether it is a change; or whether to panic or to respond in ways that are appropriate to what actual data shows about the situation. Then, understanding variation helps them to improve the system by reducing the amount of variation that seems to be occurring in it. The principle of variation can be applied to situations such as the following:

- A decline in numbers of lunches purchased by students
  —Panic: "They aren't eating right."
  —Actual data: Students prefer not to buy lunch on the days when the choir meets at lunch; they bring their lunches from home on that day.
- Changes in attendance at extra-curricular activities
  —Panic: "School spirit isn't what it used to be!"
  —Actual data: More students must ride buses that leave at dismissal time.

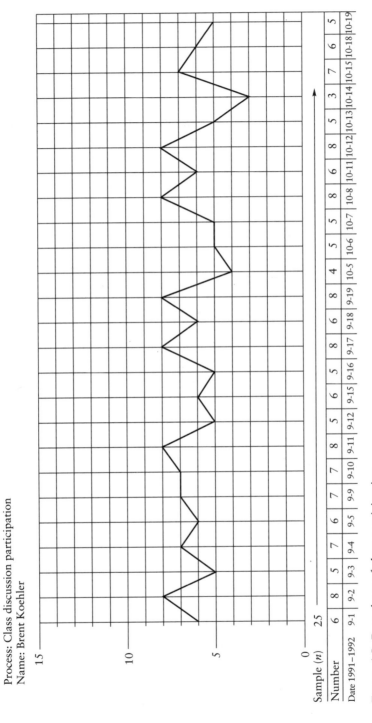

Figure 4.3: Run chart of class participation.

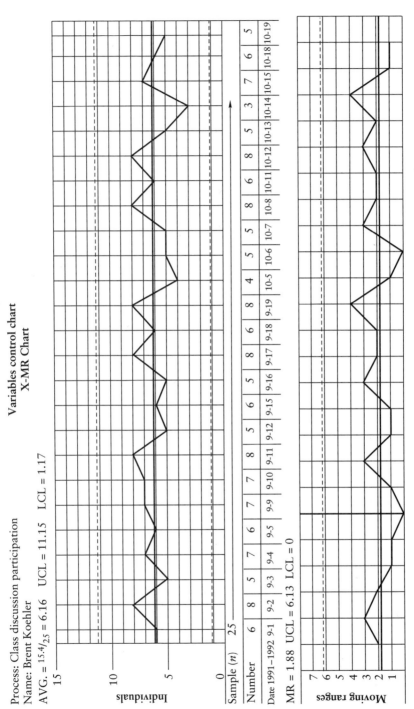

Figure 4.4: Control chart of class participation.

- Increased number of disciplinary reports
  —Panic: "Students have less self-control than they used to."
  —Actual data: The numbers of reports have not increased over time; they always tend to go up, however, in the spring term.
- Increased absenteeism of staff members
  —Panic: "When I was in school, teachers were never absent."
  —Actual data: The only increase in absenteeism has occurred as a result of increased attendance at professional conferences.
- Increased numbers of cars in the parking lot
  —Panic: "We'll have to expand the parking facility."
  —Actual data: Public transportation was disrupted by flooding, so more students and teachers have been driving for the past four months.
- Increased numbers of children riding after-school day care buses
  —Panic: "Why don't parents pick their kids up like they used to?"
  —Actual data: Parents are riding public transportation to work to save energy, and are relying on bus service for their children as well.
- Decline in number of library books checked out by young people
  —Panic: "They don't read the way they used to."
  —Actual data: Students have been purchasing books from a parents' organization special sale rather than using the library as their only source of reading materials.
- More frequent replacement of art supplies
  —Panic: "Are students stealing the crayons?"
  —Actual data: Fine arts exhibits for students at all levels have created a flurry of interest in creating art.
- Increased number of copies made on school copier
  —Panic: "Teachers are probably using the school's copier for their church and other volunteer and personal needs."
  —Actual data: Teachers are using a wider range of materials to reach their students with different approaches to their learning styles.
- Late delivery of textbook orders
  —Panic: "The business office staff never orders my books in time."
  —Actual data: Book orders have been entered at the same time each year, but increased demand has slowed down production at the publishers.

It is clear that without analysis of actual data (how many book orders were late, what is the pattern of library usage over time, and so on), the propensity is often to blame someone or arrive at sweeping conclusions that have little to do with fact. Responses based on guesses rather than on data are inappropriate, expensive, and wasteful. Furthermore, this tendency produces not only an inability to improve the situation as it exists, but undermines morale and saps energy at the same time.

Again, an understanding of variation and its relationship to stability in a system is key to managing that system. This is particularly true when dealing with a system of people. As will be seen in chapter 8, it is the responsibility of the leadership in an organization to instill an appreciation of systems and an understanding of customers. It is also the responsibility of that leadership to impart an understanding of variation in systems. This understanding involves a recognition of common and special cause variation, so that an organization can work to improve its systems.

Genuine and lasting improvement occurs when people in a system feel that they can indeed improve the system itself, without being blamed for its limitations or held accountable for its failures. As will be seen in ensuing chapters, other approaches to problem solving and statistical thinking will enhance the ability to do just that. Chapter 5 will introduce a process by which systems can be improved. When a group of students and their teacher want to do something about improving participation in classroom discussion, this process and its supporting tools will help them to do just that.

Notes

Abbott, Edwin A. [1884] 1992. *Flatland: An imaginative mathematical romance*. Reprint. New York: Dover Books.

Deming, W. Edwards. 1986. *Out of the crisis*. Cambridge, Mass.: MIT Center for Advanced Engineering Study.

A French teacher takes on control charts. 1993. Single-page insert in *Quality Toolbox* (Quality Network News of the American Association of School Administrators) 3, no. 6 (December).

Wheeler, D. J. 1993. *Understanding variation: The key to managing chaos*. Knoxville, Tenn.: SPC Press. This has a clear and complete discussion of variation.

Chapter 5

A Cycle for Learning

The real voyage of discovery consists not in seeking
new landscapes but in having new eyes.

—Marcel Proust

We all know the experience of seeing great expectations for a special dinner crumble when everything we prepare turns out to be a disaster. At that moment, all we want is a quick substitute that will save the meal and get us through the emergency. Unfortunately, this is what many people want for our educational system—which in some respects has turned into a fallen soufflé—and they may be tempted to look to quality theory, process, and tools for a solution to the disaster.

We warned you in the preface of this book that it would not give you a quick fix, and we will continue to insist that understanding quality theory, process, and tools will not eliminate the immediate emergency that some schools are experiencing. We will, however, describe in this chapter some of the elements of process; that is, what it takes to get a quality approach under way.

As schools begin the path of continuous improvement, it becomes increasingly clear that the path is indeed no quick fix to the problems that beset them. A long-term view rather than a short-term solution, it involves a repeated cycle of data collection, analysis, interpretation, evaluation, and planned change. What Deming calls the plan-do-study-act (PDSA) cycle (or the Shewhart cycle, after statistician Walter Shewhart) incorporates the elements of this process and outlines a step-by-step approach to bringing about change and improvement in any system (see Figure 5.1). An additional dimension that is vital to the success of quality in the classroom is that of evaluating improvement. As will be seen later in this chapter, traditional methods of grades and rewards can be undermining to the improvement process and destructive to learning even though they may indeed motivate students to

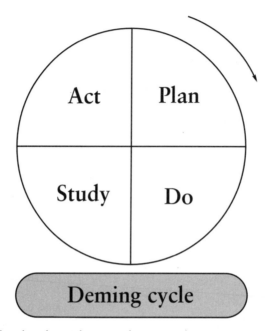

Figure 5.1: The plan-do-study-act cycle.

achieve in the classroom. Alternative methods of assessing progress are entirely consistent with improvement theory, however, and have an important place in the process of quality improvement.

Using the PDSA cycle

The plan-do-study-act approach incorporates an understanding of systems and their variation into actually changing the system to improve it. The cycle represents a powerful process to support the organization's sense of purpose and facilitate ongoing learning about that purpose and how it can become reality. This is true regardless of whether it is being utilized by the leadership of the entire school system or by a single teacher in a single classroom. Equipped with an understanding of learning theory as well as systems and their variations, a teacher (or a bus driver, or a principal) can begin to change an entire system.

A team at Bridgeview Middle School in Sidney, Ohio, responded to issues related to passage of tax levies in the district by framing a project in terms of public perception of its school. The team gathered data relating to that perception, and found that 71 percent of those surveyed felt that students were probably not entirely safe at Bridgeview Middle School. Since few disciplinary actions at the school actually related to physical safety, the team was puzzled, and even astounded, by the community's perception. Pursuing the issue further, however, the team was able to ascertain how other public image issues—appearance of the school and disorder ensuing from dismissal procedures—actually contributed to this impression.

Team members had their work cut out for them, but by using the PDSA cycle, they were able to examine their present system, collect data relating to how it was operating, make recommendations for improvement, study the ensuing changes, and ultimately standardize the improvement they had made and begin to look at ways it could be improved even more (Kume 1985). The beginning stages (plan) included defining the current system and assessing the situation. Students who participated in an affinity exercise and helped to account for root causes contributed to the solution by painting barrels to provide additional litter management around the school yard. The happy ending to the story is that the tax levy ultimately passed. While it may seem specious to attribute this passage entirely to the improvement process that the team pursued, the process itself undoubtedly contributed to enhanced community appreciation for the district. When taxpayers see teams of students, teachers, administrators, and community members working together to address problems, their response to the schools is undoubtedly positive.

Plan

The emphasis of the plan stage of the PDSA cycle is on developing knowledge about the process that is to be improved—*before* change is introduced. By means of a number of problem-solving tools, a process can be visualized, its components identified, the cause-and-effect relationships among its factors understood, and its possibilities for improvement put into focus.

Planning demands knowledge of a system's performance. Leaders responsible for improvement of the system of education will see the organization as a system. Classroom teachers and others who are responsible for subsystems and processes can identify the system of the classroom and processes within that system. A system has processes, each of which is comprised of materials, methods, environment, people, and equipment. The system of education may involve a complex matrix of processes, from orientation of new students to parent information to development of language skills to food service to classroom management. Each of these processes has the same characteristics as the larger system: the set of interrelationships among activities, people, inputs, and benefits or outputs that were previously examined.

Within a given classroom, look at the process of acquiring vocabulary skills in the context of the study of literature. Sophomore students are given a list of words that they will find in their reading of a given novel, and are expected to master these words in order to support their understanding of the literature as well as to enlarge their reading and speaking vocabularies. The teacher hopes that students will look the words up in a dictionary, record the definitions that best apply to the context of the literature, review their meaning, part of speech, and spelling, and demonstrate understanding by means of a written or oral test. This is the way that the teacher envisions the process. He or she has not necessarily checked to see if students actually pursue the process in the same way, but is aware that students usually will not look the words up until the night before the test. Some may simply copy definitions from one another and memorize them for the test. If the purpose of the system—as it often is for students—is simply to know enough for the test, this method might be considered satisfactory. But students say they want to know the words well enough that they will be able to recognize and use them on college entrance exams, and to improve their reading speed and comprehension.

A team that has been formed to improve the process of vocabulary enrichment must begin by defining the system as it exists (remember, no changes yet). Within the context of the purpose of vocabulary study, the team may come up with operational definitions of components of the system, such as vocabulary and mastery. For example, *mastery* is defined by the ability to demonstrate sufficient knowledge of the vocabulary words to be able to define and use them in sentences. In understanding the existing system of vocabulary acquisition, the team may develop a flowchart of the steps required in the process of vocabulary study (see Figure 5.2).

This example relates to a classroom situation, but the same process can also be applied to large and small systems. In the plan stage, many of the same tools and approaches can be used whether the process is applied to a scheduling problem, poor comprehension of a concept by students, chaos in the lunch line, or a purchase order system. A panoply of tools is available from which to choose, in order to document knowledge of the system. These include but are not limited to flowcharts, cause-and-effect diagrams, Pareto charts, affinity charts, run charts, check sheets, and others (see the glossary).

Once they have defined the system, the students in the vocabulary example will want to assess the situation represented in the system as it is presently operating. One tool that might be used is a cause-and-effect

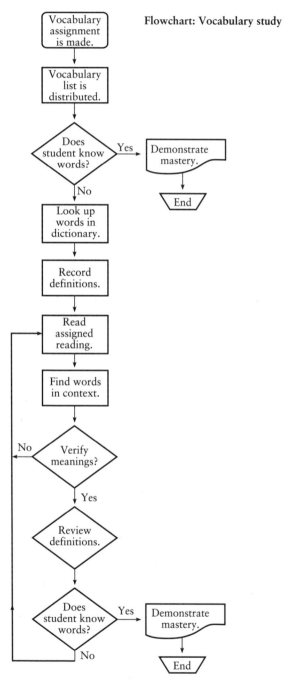

Figure 5.2: Vocabulary study flowchart.

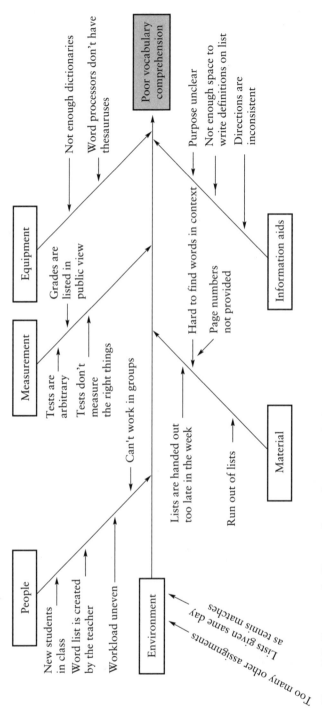

Figure 5.3: Cause-and-effect analysis of poor vocabulary comprehension.

diagram, where various causes for the outcome, "poor vocabulary comprehension," are assembled on what is known as an Ishikawa diagram, or fishbone chart. It might look like Figure 5.3.

If the measurement of improvement is to be reflected in oral and written tests over the vocabulary, the results of these tests should be assessed prior to making any changes. The number of words that students have mastered—either as individuals or as teams—might be recorded on a control chart over a period of time. Past records could be used if they have been collected in a consistent way. At least 25 data points (test scores in this case) must be used to assure that the analysis will be based on a large enough data set.

Perhaps a Pareto diagram would be useful here, in breaking down information about specific vocabulary problems that are reflected on test performance. The team might want to know, for example, what areas of vocabulary study represent the greatest challenge, such as the ability to provide antonyms, using words correctly in sentences, piecing together context clues, determining the best meaning to apply to a given context, associating words with similar meanings, and so on. A Pareto diagram or bar chart provides information about how frequently problems recur, illustrating which is the most-frequently occurring problem and which is least-frequently encountered (see Figure 5.4). It is to be noted that the Pareto diagram gives information only about the frequency of occurrence, with total cumulative percentages indicated by a line across the top of the bars. There may be other measures that should be considered as well. In considering discipline reports, for example, it may be that tardiness recurs most frequently, while assault with a

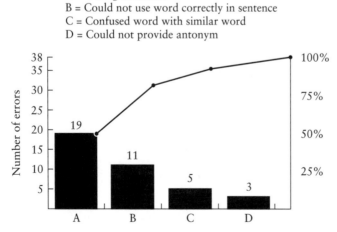

Figure 5.4: Pareto chart of vocabulary errors.

weapon may be encountered less frequently. Nonetheless, the assault cases would be treated with relatively more urgency, simply because of the seriousness of the occurrence.

Once a system is understood with respect to the way it already operates and the sources of problems in it, a team can formulate a theory for improving the system. For example, perhaps the team finds that the list of words is always given out on Wednesday, the same day that students are expected to participate in a community service project. A theory of improvement might be stated in an if-then format, with a clear sense of how the improvement will be measured. Thus,

> If weekly vocabulary lists were distributed on Mondays, then students' comprehension would be enhanced, as measured by oral and written tests.

Do

The next step is the do stage of the PDSA cycle. The improvement theory is tested over a period of time, with data collected on a regular basis so that the results can be studied. Again, a number of tools are available to support this process, but it is not our purpose here to provide instruction in their specific application. Teams will continue to analyze outcomes with control charts, histograms, force field analysis, and other tools.

Students' ability to recognize and use the words that they have found in their reading can provide a source of data to be collected and analyzed for improvement. It is important to make small, measurable changes, especially in the first experience of the improvement process. If a team attempts a complex problem with many ramifications, or one that can not be adequately measured, it will find the results to be less than satisfactory. Especially for a first experience, select a relatively simple problem to approach (not, as one Ohio district wanted to do, a scheduling problem that had been accruing complexity for years). If students try to change too many things at once—the day of the test, the way words are looked up in groups, the process of recording definitions, and the usefulness of the words with respect to SATs, for example—they will find themselves not only overwhelmed with data, but also unable to see a clear connection between a single change in the system and the ensuing improvement.

Study

In the study phase of the PDSA cycle, data can be evaluated for indications of improvement. For example, a control chart might be used to record weekly vocabulary scores in the same way that the data had been posted prior to making the recommended change in the system. A comparison can be made by using this vital tool. Say that the small change that was made in distributing the lists each week paid off in improved oral test scores. That information can be broken down and analyzed further, with the help of histograms, Pareto diagrams, and other tools.

Act

The last stage of the PDSA cycle is act. After the changes have been carefully observed and analyzed, the improvement should be standardized or implemented. Observation and analysis, however, should not end at that point. A system must be continually monitored to assure that improvements are consistently applied and to suggest other improvements that can be made. In this way, what is known as continuous improvement will come about, since the system will be revisited time and again for potential improvement. Although vocabulary mastery may have improved, for example, the team may want to assess the new situation, formulate a new theory for improvement, try it out, study the results, and standardize a new change.

Getting to the causes of problems in schools is often much more difficult than it sounds; it represents a challenge to the leadership of the organization as well as to its members. The PDSA cycle helps teams of students, teachers, administrators, parents, school board members, and others to focus on causes of problems rather than on sources for blame.

For example, attendance and tardiness are often major problems in schools. Getting students to class on time has always been a concern, for clear reasons. When a student is tardy, the dynamics of the classroom are altered or even disrupted. Every teacher knows how much time is occupied in faculty meetings discussing the kind of abuses that tardiness represents, and the appropriate response to this discipline problem. Do three or four tardies equal an absence? If a student is detained by another teacher, who is accountable for that tardy? This issue, and others like it, have been debated thousands of times by faculties from elementary schools to universities, and every conceivable kind of penalty has been implemented. In the case of tardiness as with other behavior, policies are often devised to deal only with the exception. Most students are not tardy. Most teachers dress appropriately. Most reports are turned in on time. Most employees do not lie about sick days. Rather than address the special causes in systems as special causes, organizations simply make rules to deal with them as if they are common causes. (An understanding of system variation, as we have seen, can ameliorate this tendency.)

Having the confidence to involve students in the process of improvement will change the outcome regardless of what else is done. Schools only rarely involve students in solving or monitoring problems. But after all, there is little reason for anyone to become more than mildly interested in responding to elaborate systems over which they have no control. And when they have not been involved in the design of those systems, they can freely blame someone else for the outcome.

At Mt. Edgecumbe High School in Sitka, Alaska, the question of tardiness was undertaken as an area of opportunity to address. Students were involved from the beginning, and the group pursued a seven-step improvement process. After collecting data and studying it, a plan was put into place that would serve to decrease the number of tardies. That plan was monitored and studied, and further attention was given to the improvement theory. An effort was launched to determine some of the root causes for student tardiness. A cause-and-effect diagram helped in this process, illustrating causes and their relationships to the problem. Some causes were entirely outside of student control, such as the fact that the hamburger line was longest in the school cafeteria, assuring a long wait for many students and possible lateness to after-lunch classes.

What emerges in any discussion of the improvement process is the traditional tendency to assess blame for problems, and then to determine appropriate punishments. A related issue is the sticky business of evaluating outcomes in such a way that the assessment of progress does not become either an end in itself, or a source of demoralizing punishment to students. This is particularly true in the classroom, where traditional grading practices fall into this category.

The harmful practice of grading

Long after students can recall a fourth declension Latin noun, they will remember the impact of the grades they have received in a classroom, especially when poor performance has become a pattern for them. This may be because the grades became ends in themselves; that is, sources for extrinsic rather than intrinsic motivation for improvement.

In pursuing the PDSA improvement cycle, it is clear that if team members were graded at intervals for their contributions to the process, the process itself would be seriously undermined. If they all got As for changing the vocabulary system, there would be little incentive for continuing to improve it, or for acknowledging that the improvements that have been made were not working well. Look at this important dimension of school life and its impact on the learning process.

The theory of grading as a way to measure student progress is a late development. For most of history, this theory would have been considered alien, and even counterproductive to learning. Great teachers like Socrates or Thomas Aquinas were known for dialogue with their students, not high achievement test scores. Grading and its tenuous connection to excellence derives from the factory model of competition: The worker who turns out the most widgets, the salesperson who sells the greatest number of cars, and the student who garners the highest GPA are universally rewarded and praised.

Yet a major impediment to cooperation in the classroom is that of competition fostered by the grading system. In industry, Deming (1986) points to the difficulty of expecting staff areas to work together for the good of the company, because of the evaluation of individual performance that always looms. In the same way, students are continually reminded that their own individual performances will be ranked and graded, and sometimes, that if one is to get a high grade, someone else must receive a lower grade. Students' own assessment of their progress is always colored by the expectation of the evaluation that comes from someone else. So, as every teacher knows, although it is far more productive and empowering for students to evaluate themselves than for someone else to evaluate them, the system of grading students does not allow for the potential of self-evaluation to be fully utilized in performance improvement. Many times, what people know about themselves is more accurate than the measurement provided by tests and external evaluation (Deming 1991). Students' positive judgment of themselves and their performances is often seen as inappropriate, and is discouraged by every aspect of school systems.

The rhythm of learning

Learning theorists reinforce the fact that there are different stages of learning and different purposes in learning tasks. Alfred North Whitehead (1929) identified these as "romance," where learners become fascinated in their first apprehension or experience with an idea or concept; "precision," when they learn "exactness of formulation," involving the language and discipline related to expressing themselves about that concept; and "generalization," when they are able to integrate the idea into other experiences and comprehend their implications on a general level. In this third stage, there is a return to romance, but classified ideas and techniques bring a kind of fruition to the thinking. Precision without romance, Whitehead points out, is "barren." Students who observe the beauty of nature benefit from learning scientific nomenclature to describe it, and, in the process, develop a full appreciation for natural phenomena as well as an ability to dialogue with others about what they all have observed.

Sometimes, however, classroom learning emphasizes only the precision aspect of learning. Memorizing terminology, learning definitions from memory, and acquiring appropriate vocabulary all have a place in the learning spectrum, but they do not represent the entire learning process. In fact, when students are introduced to these tasks without having developed an interest or a sense of romance in the larger ideas that they represent, then the students are doomed to boredom, if not failure. The only way that students can be inspired to participate at that point is through the system of rewards and punishments. If teachers were to summarize the kinds of questions that students ask most frequently, they would probably come down to three: Will this be on the test? Do I have to know this? and Does this count?

While working on a term paper, for example, students are often initially enthralled by a particular topic. Disciplined research enhances understanding of that topic, and producing the product of the research demonstrates an understanding of it and provides a basis for further exploration of the topic—perhaps even a lifelong interest in it. Frequently, however, the cycle is destroyed when the research outcome is graded. Some would suggest that grades provide a system of motivation, but since experiences with poor grades seem to undermine self-confidence and build defeatist attitudes, it would seem that this is not true. In fact, research suggests that the only grades that are motivating are good grades (Evans 1976, 30–50). The only students who are motivated by grades are students who are already getting the highest grades. And even the expression *good grades* is relative. The *A* student considers anything less than an *A* to be nothing short of failure. The *C* student, knowing this, may be pleased by the improvement that a *B* represents, but is unwilling to admit that to the *A* student. The *B* becomes a source of discouragement to both students.

As they become victims of a grading system that they perceive to be unfair or misleading, students often learn to put less effort into their work, and to avoid the defeat that comes with grades. "Is this right?" they ask, wondering whether their work will reflect what the teacher wants, without regard for its learning.

Another alternative is to focus only on the precision stage of the learning cycle. Memorizing, reviewing chapter questions, and doing well on in-class tests may net good grades for young people without having anything to do with the larger system of learning. Grading actually interferes with what Whitehead (1929) called the "rhythm of education," a principle that states that students should experience different modes of learning and be exposed to different subjects and ideas "at fitting times when they have reached the proper stage of mental development." The Procrustean technique of assigning grades without respect for this proper stage undermines learning and robs students of joy in their work.

Determining intrinsic value

An American exchange student who had attended a *gymnasium* in Denmark remarked about his classmates' diligence with homework. "They all do their homework every day, *even though the teacher never looks at it,*" he commented with amazement. These students prepared their work because they knew that the homework contributed to their understanding of the subject matter, not because they would be evaluated for their performance. In the American student's own experience, students completed homework because it contributed to their grades, not just because of the learning experience it might represent—for the extrinsic, rather than the intrinsic reward.

Students always seem to have time to pursue activities where they will indeed feel satisfaction and reward. Some turn to athletics, community service, drama, woodworking, art, or music. Although these activities are generally not graded, they provide intrinsic rewards and fundamental motivation for continuous improvement. Good never seems good enough when there is joy in learning. Frequent celebrations of incremental success inspire continued desire to succeed. Classroom learning, often devoid of this kind of inspiration, might take a lesson from those activities where students indeed find joy in their work.

One of the lessons of activities where students seem motivated to succeed is that of teamwork, as will be seen in chapter 6. In the case of music, for example, improvement is, in a sense, highly individual, and goals are personal ones, where each student is aiming for the next plateau in the acquisition of skills and experience. Nonetheless, individual students-performers observe that when their own skills are combined with those of other students who are all playing at levels commensurate to their own abilities, and are led by a manager (conductor) skilled at promoting and fostering cooperation, they can all combine to play at a quality level far surpassing the ability of any one individual. This synergy speaks eloquently, as has been seen, to the dramatic possibilities that teamwork holds for success in learning. These possibilities are undermined when students compete with one another for limited rewards.

The question that needs to be asked is how to motivate students to work at the same high-quality level in English, math, and science as that which they produce on the athletic field or in the rehearsal hall. Extracurricular activities are never graded, yet we consistently see students devote massive amounts of effort and garner outstanding results. Why is this?

At Mt. Edgecumbe High School, science teachers wondered what it would be like for students to approach science in the same way that coaches and players approach basketball. The result? Students designed and built a remote-controlled basketball robot called Ronnie Rust, utilizing skills learned in the lab and from the school's electrician. They wrote a report about their design and expectations, and ultimately staged a competition in which Ronnie would challenge the best of the girls' and boys' basketball teams to a shoot-out in the school gym. With a 75 percent accuracy rate in shooting from anywhere in the three-point area, Ronnie beat the basketball players hands down. The students were eager to challenge other schools to design their own basketball robots. Their enthusiasm for the project was reflected not only in the success of their product, but also in the quality of their written reports, their presentations to others about their project, their confidence in their own skills, and above all, their excitement for the learning that had taken place. They received no grades for their project.

Classroom systems often depend on grades for motivating students to perform what teachers hope will be quality work. The grading system, meant to produce symbolic indicators of student performance, instead becomes a system of punishment or reward for every task, without consideration for normal variation in output or performance (see chapter 4). Students' need to avoid punishment overrides their intrinsic need or desire to learn. Students become dependent on a teacher to dictate the required prescription for achieving a set grade. This concept is rationalized by saying that everyone has an equal chance to receive a top grade. In a perfect world without variation this would be true, but in this world it is not. As has been seen, natural variation will occur in all processes. Certainly student performance—both individual and group—will reflect the same variation. In the learning process, the variation may be even more clear than in other processes, since students will often struggle with concepts or skills in order to master them. Neither the raw material nor the finished product in the learning process will be entirely predictable nor completely finished.

System factors affect outcomes

In the workplace, quotas are often set for employees, whose performances are then rated or graded according to their ability to meet the quotas. In fact, that ability may depend on factors entirely outside the workers' control. Car sales are affected by seasonal employment, world economics, availability of options, inherent quality of the car, a dealer's willingness to discount prices, and a host of other factors that an individual salesperson cannot control. Nonetheless, he or she may be paid on the basis of such factors, and recognized for success when that success may have had little to do with individual merit. Teachers who receive merit pay based on arbitrary measurement of student achievement deny the input of all those who have contributed to that achievement level, not only throughout the students' life, but also within the current school environment. Teachers, for example, may be supported in doing a good job because other teachers work in small groups with students having difficulty in the classroom, or because colleagues have suggested specific techniques that work with students. Countless other sources of support for success can be cited as well.

The assumption of parents, teachers, and students is that grades do provide a fair assessment of progress. They may actually provide a measure only of the teachers' progress, but grades are rarely viewed from that perspective. The grades, however, are significantly influenced by the past experiences of the people doing the rating. Students quickly ascertain that the apparent goal is to find out what the raters want, and then to do it. As long as the goal is only one of meeting the teachers' standards, this system works. When there are other objectives to be gained, grades are not only unsupportive, but they are also destructive to such goals as working for the joy of learning, pride of workmanship, and continuous improvement. To the student who gets an A, there is little incentive to examine ways to improve. To the student who gets an F, certainly there is little motive even to try.

Customary grading of students, performance rating of teachers, and evaluation of employees are all tactics that serve to limit the very productivity that they were instituted to promote. At the same time they suboptimize the overall system. People need feedback on how to improve, but they do not need to be judged. Since a manager/teacher cannot tell who in the system will learn any given subject, process, or fact quickly, rating employees and students against each other only degrades their attempts and diminishes the risks they are willing to take. Because schools deal with young people with varying rates and at various levels of development, judging students at any given point in their development signals to these students that they are considered successes or failures—often at very young ages. The self-fulfilling prophesy is a powerful shaper of expectations in life (Merton 1968).

Seen from the point of view of variation, some students will indeed fall outside the control limits of a standard learning system. These can be addressed as special causes and receive the attention they need. At the same time, students and teachers can work together to improve the entire system and to minimize variation in the system. Classroom systems in which student output is graded by teachers and recorded, and then—regardless of the result—the class moves on, are destructive not only to the individual's learning, but also to the hope for improvement of the system itself. Grades are not a measure of student performance, but a measure of the managers' ability to predict future success. Removing grades or at least the competitive threat of grades removes fear of failure and helps to restore the joy of learning that begins to erode from the time the five-year-old enters the system.

Learning from failures

Why is it so important to remove the fear of failure? Without failure, improvement is limited. All great discoveries are made through successive failures—even catastrophic failure. Penicillin, after all, was discovered through the failure of a previous experiment. Thomas Edison once had many scientists working on a particularly difficult problem. After 22 different ways of attacking the problem, he was approached by one of the scientists who was in favor of giving up the experiment as impossible. Edison replied that the experiment had not been a failure at all; that it had clearly demonstrated 22 ways that did not work, and those would not have to be tried again. *Failure* to Edison meant *discovery*. If the experiments had been teacher-graded, however, they probably would not have led to the ultimate success that they produced. *Fail forward,* a concept that emphasizes learning from setbacks, provides a key foundation for quality learning.

Fostering a system where students will take appropriate risks in their learning processes, feel good about the steps they take toward improvement, and increase their ability to evaluate their own work, supports the aim of the school with respect to developing a love of learning and the ability to learn successfully throughout life. This goal can be accomplished without the use of grades as bribes or punishments, as Kohn (1993) emphasizes.

It cannot be done, however, without the use of appropriate evaluation, involving feedback but not rating. Students must have a sense of how to improve, if that improvement is to actually take place. Teachers who are facilitating the process of improvement have the responsibility of developing a feedback system that will support the students' need to know how they are doing. Dismantling the grading process does not mean discarding evaluation systems. Ongoing evaluation is critical to improvement, but alternative methods of assessment provide support to the improvement process in ways that grades cannot.

Alternatives to grading

Viable alternatives to the practice of grading students are being used with success in many school settings. What is known as *authentic as-*

sessment is a way for students to test what they have learned in a given situation, and to base learning on forms of work that reflect real-life situations. Mark Twain Elementary School, in Littleton, Colorado, and Urbandale High School in Urbandale, Iowa, for example, have received attention for their approaches to authentic assessment (National Center for Effective Schools Research and Development 1991).

Elementary teachers have used portfolio evaluation for several years, as will be seen. This strategy involves keeping portfolios of actual work: papers that have been written, artwork that has been created, and problems that have been solved. Teachers and learners regularly review the portfolio to determine student needs and to develop strategies for further needs. Group sessions offer additional opportunities for learners to support each other's improvement.

Tests, too, can be appropriately used to measure student progress. Prepared presentations can demonstrate how well students understand something. Knowing what methods, environment, tools, and people to involve in evaluation is the teachers' responsibility. One teacher says it is important to read student papers closely and note weaknesses carefully so she will be able to improve her own teaching of writing skills. While this is useful for the teacher's needs, the process must accommodate student needs as well. Students must be involved in the evaluation of their work in order to take ownership of the improvement process. This can be brought about in incremental ways by creating opportunities for students to select their best work, for example, or to work with a writing partner to improve both students' work. When parents are invited for conferences, the students themselves can walk their parents through the progress represented in the portfolio.

Teachers who prepare their classrooms for parent open houses often display student work that will reflect the quality of the learning experience. These teachers do not post standardized tests or other measures of success, but instead exhibit actual student work. Often they will make an effort to provide examples of every student's work, selecting the best from each child's portfolio. This exhibit will communicate quality of work far more clearly than any number of standardized tests can do, and, at the same time, it will help students to feel pride in what they have created. This exhibit is a kind of demonstration of how well students have mastered skills and concepts. When parents see their children's best work, they participate in the pride that each child feels about doing well.

To be successful in the learning process, students must be able to demonstrate what they know, and must understand how they know that they know. All students will not be at the same point at a given moment. When the purpose of a class is to develop competence with conversational Spanish, students will not only acquire this competence at different rates, but they will learn in different ways. As will be seen in chapter 7, classrooms that accommodate an understanding of the seven intelligences and brain-based learning theory will provide for these differences. At a given moment, for example, some students may be ready to practice their dialogues with other students; others will be studying the vocabulary that they will need for their conversations; and a few may respond to taped models of conversations to enhance their sense of the language's cadence. A teacher's role will be to help students identify the most appropriate learning opportunity for their needs.

But how will these students be evaluated? The shortcomings of a written test in this situation are clear. Students could conceivably write a perfect conversation without ever being able to speak a word of it. If the objective is to carry on a conversation, the appropriate evaluation instrument would certainly involve doing just that. Students might prepare conversations in small groups or they might demonstrate their mastery by delivering a speech or by impromptu responses to questions. A written test of vocabulary might support the objective of learning to speak Spanish, but it is no substitute for actually speaking it when it comes to evaluating the success of the process. Every language teacher knows that—without a single grade being given—an entire classroom of students could demonstrate for their classmates, their teacher, and themselves how well they have met the challenge of speaking Spanish at the level they have mastered. "I have been astounded at the honesty and fairness with which students can judge their own work," says Leander, Texas, art teacher Dianne Matheny.

Communicating achievement

Of course, communicating a level of achievement is another function of the grading system. Grades have provided a useful tool not only for attempting to motivate students, but also for communicating successes and failures to parents and other customers. Theoretically, a prospective employer can feel confident that if students have earned an *A,* they can demonstrate an excellent grasp of concepts or knowledge. As most of us know, however, this is not the case. The high grade may have little to do with mastery, and a low grade may have nothing to do with the potential for success. A University of California mathematics professor who had taught beginning calculus reported with amazement that his students had come to him with close-to-4.0 grade point averages in their high school programs, and yet many could not do the simplest calculations in mathematics, and seemed incapable of higher-order analytical skills. Grade inflation has exacerbated the already-limited capacity for GPAs to communicate information. Teachers are often afraid to fail students because of the challenges the teachers will face from parents, administrators, and even at times the legal system.

Grades, in fact, represent a highly limited vehicle for communication of student progress. A teacher tells of a parent who made an appointment to discuss a student's grade on an English paper. "I just want to know why Mark got a *B* on this paper," the parent demanded.

"Because it was a *very good* paper," was the teacher's response. An exact and objective measure—the *B*—communicated entirely different things to the teacher and to this parent. It will likewise communicate different messages from one school to another and from one classroom to another.

Paul Dressel (1957, 6) called grades "an inadequate report of an inaccurate judgment by a biased and variable judge of the extent to which a student has attained an undefined level of mastery of an unknown proportion of an indefinite amount of material." If students, parents, prospective employers, university admissions officers, and other school customers want to know how well students have mastered certain concepts or understandings, it is important that this information be communicated in a way that will be clearly understood and meaningful. Grades alone cannot do this.

Portfolio assessments

Successes with ongoing evaluation of portfolio work have demonstrated that there are indeed other ways to approach evaluation and important feedback relating to progress. Students whose written work is maintained in folders where they can revisit it, evaluate it, improve any of it, discuss it with a teacher, share it with classmates, and take note of areas of improvement, are certain to see improvement that can never be generated by means of arbitrary numerical grades on essays. How can students possibly know how to begin to improve an essay that has been judged to be an 85, to one that might be considered an 87?

In the Pittsburgh public schools, where portfolio assessments have been utilized for several years, a foundation officer noted that the portfolio represented a far more accurate reflection of how young people are meeting the challenge of writing than other measures he had seen. Increasingly, individual schools and even state education systems are adopting the portfolio assessment as a viable way of demonstrating student mastery of writing skills, in particular. Portfolios have the advantage of communicating not only to students, but also to observers, for the portfolios represent authentic work that students have created. Furthermore, a study funded by the National Science Foundation suggested that the six major standardized achievement tests, as well as tests that supplement textbooks, drive instruction toward lower-level knowledge and skills, instead of supporting higher-order abilities (Rothman 1992).

In another example, a portfolio system developed by kindergarten teachers Kristi Tindell and Sharon Calvin for their Whitestone Elementary School in Leander, Texas, classroom includes the following:

- Results of kindergarten prescreening tests done at the beginning of the year
- Photos of children in costumes, acting in plays, and working on projects
- Audiocassettes of children singing, reading, or playacting in dramas
- Journals with writing assessment, drawings, other writing samples (including the child's name in his or her handwriting)
- Affective assessments such as student interest inventory, reading habits, and surveys
- Classroom observations by teachers and others of speaking, listening, writing, and reading, including anecdotal records and checklists
- Theme projects and assessments based on goals for different units
- Report cards

The contents of these portfolios can communicate far more to the children, parents, and teachers than any rating scale or grade can. Further, the process of gathering portfolio data and sharing it with students helps young people to evaluate the quality of their work, and provides a basis for enhanced pride in workmanship. While grading and ranking are in a way easier for teachers than the kind of constant vigilance that this system demands, it draws on the teachers' professional preparation as caring facilitators of learning rather than demanding skills for documentation to support arbitrary judgments about the quality of students' work.

Student role in assessment

Open-ended assessment practices and other methods that are closer to students' classroom experiences than grades have garnered increased interest, although there is no common agreement about these methods. Performance sampling, including portfolio evaluation, represents a collection of documents reflecting student writing, computations, and drawing. Sometimes students rank all of the papers in their individual files, from weakest to strongest, without grades. This exercise not only helps students learn to carefully scrutinize their own work and evaluate its quality, but also gives them a genuine source of pride in their work. Even the youngest students know when they have done their best work or when it has been done quickly or carelessly. When this evaluation is made only by teachers, it is far less likely to have an impact on improvement than when students do it themselves.

Tests, another form of evaluation, help teachers to check up on learning at a given point in time. Tests provide information that will help teachers evaluate the system itself; that is, how well the classroom managed by the teacher is working. Tests can also help students evaluate how well they are gaining mastery in a particular area and give direction to next steps in the learning process. Tests serve as tools to demonstrate learning and are by no means to be considered useless. It is only when they are used within a system of rewards and punishments that tests are harmful. Teachers monitor student progress and performance in a variety of ways. At the same time, tests can help students themselves to evaluate their own learning. Feedback from tests, from teacher conferences, from peers, and from the students' own observations are valuable in helping young people gain a sense of how well they are learning. It is critical that the assessment take place in a variety of formats and environments, in order to give students information not only about the outcome of their work, but also about the process.

Jane Delaney, a science teacher at Leander (Texas) High School, is using quality learning methods in her classroom. She notes that her students "used to take a test, earn a grade, and that was it." With new emphasis on knowing what they know and how they know it, the same students now take tests, earn grades, and then improve their learning and their grades. Students who want to improve their tests can make corrections, then sign up for individual interviews, where they explain the processes or concepts that were tested and demonstrate application of their learning. The focus has shifted from the grade to the learning that the grade was meant to reflect, a first step to begin to bridge from a totally extrinsic system of reward to that which derives satisfaction from intrinsic rewards.

In the same school system, Maureen Chase uses oral language tests to evaluate growth in fifth-grade language skills. Students keep run charts of their weekly grades on these tests, then analyze their charts for patterns, and make decisions about how they can improve their language progress.

Competency matrices

Another approach to the problem of evaluating and communicating information is that of the learning competency matrix (see Figure 5.5). A chart of progress with respect to key learning objectives, the matrix provides a way for students and teachers to have ready access to students' learning processes. In the example, students who are studying skills of journalism will have different levels of understanding for a variety of course outcomes. Clearly, a single grade cannot communicate these differences, but the learning matrix can.

Using Bloom's taxonomy (Bloom et al. 1956) as a basis, the matrix asks students and teachers to evaluate the kind of learning that students have at a given point. Of course, students will be asked to demonstrate their knowledge ("How do I know that I know?") so that the matrix reflects a realistic assessment of progress. At this point, a student may have given an oral report about news reporting. The teacher and the student agree that the report reflected knowledge, understanding, and thinking skills such as application and analysis. The student would fill in the chart to this point. The student becomes increasingly aware that learning is not binomial ("I either know it or I don't know it"), but progressive and dynamic.

In another area, perhaps demonstrating expanded vocabulary, students may have taken a short quiz on a list of words, demonstrating their knowledge of the language, the first level of competence. Not ready to demonstrate further understandings of the vocabulary, students would fill in only the first level of the matrix.

When all of the outcomes of a course or program are listed, and students' progress is charted with respect to these outcomes rather than to some arbitrary standard for the course, not only students but also teachers, administrators, parents, and external customers will have a clear understanding of student progress. The chart represents a kind of map of students' learning at any given moment. It also diminishes dichotomous interpretation of learning to which students often succumb. Instead of communicating "I learned it" or "I didn't," the matrix suggests the ways in which students have grown in their understanding or skill level.

A further effect of utilizing such a vehicle for evaluation and communication about progress is that students understand that they are never finished. An excellent grade in a course, on the other hand, may communicate to students that there is nothing further for them to learn in that subject—surely a misleading and destructive idea in lifelong learning.

The learning competency matrix also encourages students to learn from failures. Failure puts them on the brink of discovery. With teachers watching this failure, ready to stamp it with a grade, students will opt for the safer way, which may involve mere imitation of the teacher model or short-term memorization to prepare for tests. When students are brought to the brink of discovery, they have joy in what they learn. It is to be emphasized that grades should never be given for achieving

Name _____

Beginning date _____

Cumulative learning evaluation summary
Journalism 1

Outcomes	Competencies:	Level I Knowledge	Level II Understanding/ comprehension	Level III Application	Level IV Analysis	Level V Synthesis	Level VI Appreciation/ evaluation
	Triangle: elements of news						
	Facts and news						
	Elements of interest in news						
	Inverted pyramid						
	Leads						
Write news article	Purpose						
	Length						
	Content						
	5Ws and H						
	Kinds						
	Interviews						
Communicate effectively in writing	Setting up the interview						
	Questioning techniques						
	Quoting accurately						
	Using lead–transition, quote–transition, and so on						
	Attribution						
	Headlines						
	Purpose						
	Style						
	Content						
	Editing news						
	Proofreading						
	Being concise						
	Developing clarity						

Figure 5.5: Langford competency matrix (adapted for The Miami Valley School journalism class).

higher levels—a practice that blurs students' ability to clearly see their growth.

A simplified version of the matrix was developed by teacher Anne Treviño, at Block House Creek Elementary School in Leander, Texas. Even young children can evaluate their own learning and record progress on these charts (see Figure 5.6).

Informal assessments of progress

In elementary-level classrooms, ongoing assessment that provides information about each child's growth is often easy to discern. By reading a story to children, teachers carry on a dialogue with their students and assess their understanding of character, plot, and details of setting. Children are given opportunities to select books for their own reading, either from classroom shelves or the school library. Teachers will note the children's selections and observe their attention span and interest during quiet reading time. The class may go on to creating a play or making costumes about a book they have read together. Again, teachers observe each child's skills and leadership roles in group activity (Perrone 1991).

Competency matrix

Please write the activity, goal, or objective below. Shade in the boxes that apply.	Did I hear it? 	Do I understand it? 	Could I use it? 	Could I explain it? 	Could I teach it? 	Could I grade or evaluate it? 

Figure 5.6: Learning matrix for grades K–5 music classes (developed by Anne Treviño, Leander, Texas).

When teachers are making these observations or discussing a child's progress with the child, other teachers, or the parents, the communication can take place without any reference to grades. In fact, the parent conference is perhaps the best opportunity for teachers to provide anecdotal information and observation that communicate a child's learning patterns. Since, as will be observed in chapter 7, student learning in a classroom of young people does not happen at the same time and in the same way (any more than their physical growth patterns are identical), it is essential that this communication be couched in terms of the student's own learning rather than how well that learning stacks up against others' progress.

In the secondary school, it is equally essential to communicate accurately to students about the learning process. By the time students are in high school, it is clear that they can observe not only what is learned, but also how it is learned. Students can develop authentic ways to demonstrate or evaluate mastery of concepts and skills for themselves in fairly sophisticated ways. Leander High School science teacher Jim Genty uses a variety of student self-assessments to evaluate students' levels of understanding of physics. He facilitates class discussions about the learning process. "Students enjoy talking about school because it is something they have lived every day since they were six years old. They get excited about learning when they feel they can be part of the process," he says. Genty combines the use of a learning matrix with individual interviews, where he sees students' ownership of the learning process reflected in their observations about their progress. Continuous improvement cannot be sustained without continuous communication about quality. This communication is enhanced not only by face-to-face conferences, but also through tools and processes that help students see their progress and direct their further learning.

Teachers have always recognized the limitations of grades; they often find the evaluation process that the grading system represents to be the least satisfying aspect of their jobs. Educators recognize the barrier of resentment that is often created when students perceive that teachers have given a particular grade. Even when teachers are "required" to record grades for their students, reflecting on the need for evaluation of learning and creating new processes of communication can minimize the negative impact of the grading process. For example, students can participate in mutually agreed-on criteria upon which grades will be based.

Using alternative assessments when grades are required

Monta Akin is assistant superintendent of instruction for the Leander Independent School District, where the board of education policy requires that numerical grades be given from second grade on. Akin supports teachers' methods to involve students in the process of self-evaluation that help to shift students' attitudes from "What grade did the teacher give me?" to "What grade did I earn?" Some of these methods—portfolio assessment, students charting their progress, interviews, and conferences—have been examined in this chapter. Certainly teachers can be considered managers of the systems that are represented in their classrooms. As managers, they can continue to work to improve the system of evaluation as it relates to the system of learning that the school itself supports.

In a Miami Valley School journalism classroom, in Dayton, Ohio, students compile portfolio examples of all of their written work throughout a term, including multiple drafts of each paper they have composed. In a conference with each student, the teacher and student select samples of the student's best work and discuss the grade that the work might receive when it is assessed against the characteristics of excellent writing that they agreed on early in the term. If a hard news story lead does not have the traditional 5 Ws and an H, for example, it cannot be considered an excellent lead.

A troubling emphasis on standardized, statewide testing practices, as noted in chapter 3, is occurring at the same time that professional educators are increasingly aware of the limitations of such practices. Lawmakers and elected officials have preempted educators' professional competence in evaluating students in unprecedented ways. Imagine physicians' reactions if every diagnosis were to be measured in a statewide, numerically based, accountability search. Or if professional psychologists were required to submit tests of their patients' progress to state legislators, based on daylong testing procedures that diminished their counselling time with clients. And yet the teaching profession has indeed been subjected to such outrage, with classroom learning actually suboptimized to the testing procedures mandated by governmental agencies. Politicians with no knowledge of how learning takes place substitute arbitrary test goals for improvement in the system of learning.

In a national survey of 1200 math teachers, 80 percent noted that they had made instructional changes as a result of standardized tests administered in their districts. While teachers are aligning their methods to the tests themselves, the tests "are not aligned with the future needs of students" (Chambers 1993). The entire testing phenomenon shifts the emphasis—indeed the very purpose—of schools from the learning process to the testing process. Quality principles underscore the disservice that this practice does to students, violating fundamentals of long-term thinking, the purpose of the educational system, variation, teamwork, and management of systems. Testing for its own sake, or for the purposes of comparing outcomes among districts, is a destructive practice whether it takes place within an individual classroom or on a national scale. If classrooms did nothing else but reinvest the weeks spent preparing for and taking tests into improving the learning process itself, learning would improve.

A further dimension of the deleterious practice of comparing standardized test scores as a way of evaluating school districts is that of community makeup. Test scores, it has been suggested, have far more to do with median income in the community, for example, than with the quality of instruction within a school (Test scores tend to rise 1994).

Grading teachers

If it is true that grades "are not merely symptoms but primary causes of many learning problems" (Hargis 1990, 9), the ranking and grading of teachers undoubtedly has the same effect. Performance reviews, which often replace ongoing, regular supportive feedback and constructive suggestion about problems and successes in teaching, undermine teachers as surely as the grading process discourages their students. Merit pay, incentives tied to student performance, recognition for individual successes, and other practices that emphasize ranking and rating of teachers are destructive. Like students who worry about grades, teachers seeking help with a classroom problem will be loathe to go to a principal, who is also evaluator, for help. One teacher who did this—acknowledging candidly that she was struggling to find variety in her classroom format one year—found her "problem" referred to in performance appraisals for several years. It had given the evaluator an excuse for a lower ranking, since teachers can never receive only high marks in these systems. And her principal often said to her, "How are you doing with your classroom format problem?" Do you suppose she was likely to share her professional growth ideas as honestly in future conferences with her principal?

Another teacher who had figured out the state appraisal system for teachers well enough that she earned top marks every year, acknowledged that she was afraid to try anything new under that system, for fear that her marks would decline. When the system was no longer used in her school under a two-year waiver experiment, she remarked, "I can hardly wait to start!" Another teacher in the same system, calling the experiment the "two years without fear," commented, "Up to this point, no one had ever asked me what I wanted to learn, what I wanted to work on, what I felt was important about my job."

Grading teachers through annual performance appraisals denies an individual's role in the system. If students, teachers, parents, administrators, school board members, and others are working together to improve the entire system of education, the individual rating of any single component will be destructive to this unity. Notice that this does not deny the role of evaluation, guidance, or coaching. If a teacher is consistently late to class, the onus is on the principal or other supervisor to notice immediately and coach the teacher to improve. Waiting until June and then reporting that a teacher has been late to class 15 times serves no purpose except to destroy morale and engender bitterness.

Evaluation and learning

A process of improvement that involves looking closely at an existing system and then taking steps to enhance the performance of that system involves regular and ongoing assessment of improvement. The evaluation focuses on how well processes are working, not on the quality of individual performance within that system. When student learning is seen as a process and the aim is to improve student learning, assessment practices focus on how well the learning process is doing. Student performance is evaluated in the context of the learning system, not for the purpose of evaluation alone.

As will be seen in chapter 7, understanding learning theory and the fundamentals of brain physiology can provide a framework within which the practices of evaluation and assessment can be considered. As with all quality learning, specific educational practices must be supported by theory, rather than merely copied from others' systems or introduced out of exigency or trendiness. Each elephant is, after all, unique.

Notes

Bloom, B., M. Englehart, E. Furst, W. Hill, and D. Krathwohl, eds. 1956. *Taxonomy of educational objectives: The classification of educational goals.* New York: David McKay.

Chambers, Donald L. 1993. Standardized testing impedes reform. *Educational Leadership* 50, no. 5: 80.

Covey, Stephen R. 1989. *The seven habits of highly effective people: Powerful lessons in personal change.* New York: Simon and Schuster/Fireside Books.

Deming, W. Edwards. 1986. *Out of the crisis.* Cambridge, Mass.: MIT Center for Advanced Engineering Study.

———. 1991. The newsmakers: Outside motivation submerges joy of work, says quality guru Deming, who calls for emphasis on the individual. *Electronics* (May): 74.

Dressel, Paul L. 1957. Facts and fancy in assigning grades. *Basic College Quarterly* (Michigan State University) (winter): 6–12.

Evans, F. G. 1976. What research says about grading. In *Degrading the grading myths: A primer of alternatives to grades and marks,* edited by S. B. Simon and J. A. Bellanca. Washington, D.C.: Association for Supervision and Curriculum Development.

Hargis, Charles H. 1990. *Grades and grading practices: Obstacles to improving education and to helping at-risk students.* Springfield, Ill.: Charles C. Thomas. Hargis cites F. G. Evans. 1976. What research says about grading. In *Degrading the grading myths: A primer of alternatives to grades and marks,* edited by S. B. Simon, and J. A. Bellanca. Washington, D.C. Association for Supervision and Curriculum Development.

Kohn, Alfie. 1993. *Punished by rewards.* New York: Houghton Mifflin.

Kume, Hitoshi. 1985. *Statistical methods for quality improvement.* Tokyo: 3A Corporation.

Merton, Robert K. 1968. The self-fulfilling prophecy. In *Social theory and structure,* edited by Robert K. Merton. New York: Free Press.

National Council for Effective Schools Research and Development. 1991. Authentic assessment. *Focus in Change* (Madison: Wisconsin Center for Education Research) (March): 1.

Perrone, Vito, ed. 1991. *Expanding student assessment.* Alexandria, Va.: Association for Supervision and Curriculum Development.

Rothman, Robert. 1992. Performance-based assessment gains prominent place on research docket. *Education Week,* 4 November, 1.

Test scores tend to rise with median income. 1994. *Dayton Daily News,* 19 May.

Whitehead, Alfred North. 1929. *The aims of education and other essays.* New York: Macmillan.

Chapter 6

Cooperation: Changing the Feel of the Classroom

Cooperation must come to be seen as a fundamental orientation toward other people rather than a set of techniques that are hauled out for specific lessons. This means changing the feel of the classroom itself.

—Alfie Kohn,
No Contest: The Case Against Competition

Imagine eight suburban high school girls and their two female teachers choosing to live together for a month in the harsh winter environment of a cabin in northern Vermont, with temperatures that hover between 6 and −30 degrees Fahrenheit, while depending on a wood fire for warmth and a protected spring on the other side of the frozen lake for drinking water. What learning competencies could be garnered from such an experience?

If the possibilities were to be listed, they would undoubtedly emphasize skills of physical survival. If these young women had been dropped precipitously into this harsh setting without preparation, they would have had to determine ways in which they could survive until they might be rescued. The resourcefulness of the human spirit and its sense of cooperation virtually assure that such a group would work together to gather wood, tend the fire, carry water, and prepare meals.

With emphasis on teamwork and cooperation, this group went far beyond its original goal of survival. Among the products of the young women's experience were a collection of poems, a children's picture book, a photographic essay, a graphic fabric design, a videotaped documentary, a collection of charcoal sketches, a book shelf, a carved and finished wood sign for the Vermont camp, skits, original dances, and shared reports on the New England town meeting system, regional wildlife, historical perspectives, and cross-country ski instruction.

In addition, they planned meals and shopped for food in a town some 30 minutes away, carried wood, kept open a hole in the 24-inch ice of the lake for utility water, skied across the lake every day for drinking water, kept daily journals, scheduled daily team meetings to focus on issues, and worked on skills of communication and exercises in team development. In music and skit, they reflected on their experiences.

What is perhaps unique about this list of accomplishments is that they were not the result of assignments by teachers, but were student-driven. The students were not graded in a traditional way. They planned the best use of their time to accomplish their objectives, which had been determined by a brainstorming session that answered the question, when this course ends, how will I know it has been successful?

Not one of the criteria generated in this brainstorming included the phrase "if I get an *A*." A focus on teamwork minimizes the need for individual reward, just as eliminating a focus on individual recognition diminishes competition and enhances teamwork.

This group was part of an intensive immersion program offered by The Miami Valley School, a Dayton, Ohio independent school, where students and teachers focus on learning in nontraditional, intensive ways. The success of the learning experience in this setting is largely the outcome of teamwork and group process, not of learning directed by teachers. These students saw themselves as part of a system that would provide them with the outcomes that they had chosen for themselves. The teachers' role was one of leading, not directing. The two facilitator-leaders introduced skills of teamwork and problem solving and facilitated discussion of outcomes and ways to bring them about, using tools of problem solving and statistical analysis to help the group identify processes and understand systems.

Synergy of teams

One essential ingredient of systems thinking and the success of total quality management in any environment—industry or education—is that of teamwork. The system is made up of many individuals' contributions, and is enhanced by their working together. The synergy that results from this cooperation is well documented. Students in the Vermont course, for example, worked together to create a bookshelf, using one student's gift for detail, another's creative flair, and another's logical approach. None did more than another, for they saw each other's contributions as equally important in creating what they all wanted—a high-quality, well-constructed, and attractive shelf unit. (In working toward that objective, students used skills related to the subject areas of math, art, physics, and speech—or at least persuasive argument.)

An individual's ability to contribute is enhanced by the contributions of others who share the same vision in a variety of environments.

Ballet dancers sometimes rehearse their solos with other dancers, finding that the energy of two dancing in a room somehow inspires the soloist to greater performance. The second dancer is there to support the first as a teammate rather than a competitor, so that the performance of the entire company will be better. When the time comes for the soloist to dance, the second dancer is no longer needed, and has faded into the background.

Competition, however, is what Alfie Kohn (1986, 1) calls America's "number one obsession . . . the common denominator of American life." As Kohn suggests, however, we are so immersed in it that, like the fish who is no longer aware of the water in which it swims, we do not even recognize that it is one of our most important values. If this is the case, how can our students learn the value of supporting the efforts of others in order to optimize the success of the entire system? One way is by working together as teams with a shared vision of their own success.

In systems thinking, the linear, cause-effect relationship between individual decisions and the solutions to problems is replaced by a shift to an emphasis on interrelationships and "seeing *processes* of change rather than snapshots" (Senge 1990; Senge et al. 1994). The emphasis on identifying individual roles and rewarding them rather than on improving the process as a whole must change if America is to play an effective world leadership role. Our schools can do their part to bring about a shift in the paradigm of learning systems.

Of course, teamwork and a spirit of cooperation do not just happen, as any athletic coach will attest. They must be built carefully, using skills of problem solving and communication that create an atmosphere of trust and confidence. These skills can be learned in the classroom and applied in every group problem-solving activity. As they are learned and applied, teachers will observe a whole new way of thinking on the part of students, for they will begin to take responsibility for their own problem solving rather than relying on adult leadership to give answers.

Team skills

Among specific tools that can be applied to this process are *brainstorming*—a technique that is often misunderstood as a loose throwing out of ideas, when, in fact, it is a structured format for creativity, where every member of a team contributes, and all ideas are considered without ridicule or evaluation. Students at very young ages can be taught to sit in circles, consider an issue, and offer their ideas one by one, without interrupting others or criticizing their thinking. A facilitator, perhaps the teacher, will manage the process to assure that everyone speaks in turn, that the brainstorming process continues long enough to exhaust the creative thinking of the group, and that all ideas are considered. As each child offers an idea, the facilitator will record it on a large chart or chalk board where everyone can see the list that has been generated. When participants do not seem to have ideas to offer when it is their turn, they will indicate this by saying "pass" rather than by remaining silent. Look at a brainstorming activity for students in a high school literature class.

Issue: What are some reasons that Sylvia, the child in Sarah Orne Jewett's story "A White Heron," decides not to tell the ornithologist where the heron makes its nest?

Ideas, as they are presented, include the following:

- Her love of the bird
- Respect for the natural environment
- Fear of what may happen to the bird
- Sense of ownership of the secret about the bird's nest
- Concern about what the ornithologist will do next
- Hatred of men
- Sense of beauty
- Camaraderie with the bird
- (Pass)
- Pride in her own knowledge
- Friendship with the heron
- Fear of the man's intrusion
- (Pass)
- The fact that Sylvia has never told her grandmother, who might now resent that she is eschewing the reward
- The possibility that Sylvia is a radical environmentalist

Notice that in a traditional classroom format, where a teacher throws out questions and waits for the "right" answer, probably only one or two of these responses would be generated by students. The teacher would undoubtedly give immediate feedback such as "That's right," or "I think so, too." Others in the class would assume that there are no other right answers, or that their answers would not be acceptable to the teacher. In the brainstorming environment, students are encouraged to see the question from a variety of viewpoints and considerations. Since there is no immediate evaluation, the emphasis is on continuing the thinking process rather than on finding a single correct answer. The rewards include an understanding of the richness of others' responses, enhanced listening skills, and creativity engendered by percolating answers rather than taking the most obvious.

To further develop a discussion of this same story, the question might be posed in another fashion.

Issue: What are some reasons that Sylvia feels she *should* tell the ornithologist about the bird?

Possible responses include the following:

- She is attracted to him.
- There is a reward involved.
- Her grandmother is very poor and could use the money.

Finally, another problem-solving technique might be applied to the same discussion. *Force field analysis* (Ball et al. 1992) considers the forces that are moving a decision in one direction, opposing forces, and ways in which the conflict can be resolved. The idea is to determine ways to reduce the restraining forces, increase driving forces, or pursue a combination of these. Whether it is applied to a short work of fiction or a real-life problem, the technique fosters thinking skills that cannot be developed without participation and group support for all responses.

In using these and other techniques for a discussion of motivation in literature, students will find themselves

- Learning more about characterization and motivation
- Going back to the story for deeper insight and analysis
- Considering new approaches offered by others' thinking
- Understanding more about their own motivations
- Seeing complexity where they might be tempted to see simplicity
- Respecting their classmates, whose ideas they have perhaps not heard before
- Feeling that they have contributed to a discussion, rather than being a passive observer of other students who raise their hands to answer
- Seeing the teacher's role as one of facilitator of their own learning, rather than as one of knowledge-giver with the correct answer
- Developing skills of interpretation of literature

- Observing the richness of language and its ambiguities
- Understanding conflict as a fundamental aspect of the short story.

The teacher's role

Look at that list of responses to the brainstorming issue. They can't all be correct, and some of them are really off the wall. How does a teacher assure that a class doesn't go off the deep end in providing suggestions about an issue? Remember that it is sometimes the deep end responses that help students clarify their thinking and analyze something even more deeply. Naturally, if something is patently wrong or misrepresentative, a teacher will want to help students to understand that. There are ways to provide such feedback within the framework of the tool itself.

After the list has been generated, the teacher asks for clarification for each list item, making sure that each is clearly understood by all team members. The teacher may encourage discussion of the ideas in that process, in which case there will be an opportunity to correct any errors. For example, if a student had said "Sylvia's father taught her to save birds," further discussion would elicit a correction—ideally from another student, but otherwise from the teacher. The fact is, there is no evidence in the story to support this assertion, for Sylvia had been orphaned at a very young age, and her father is never mentioned in the story.

Another technique that can follow the brainstorming and can help the group to determine the most important of the ideas raised is that of the nominal group technique, illustrated in chapter 2. This tool helps a group to rank order the items listed. Again, each student will be a part of the outcome, because every student's voice is heard in the process. Nominal group technique helps teams to make better decisions, when a decision is needed. In the literature example, it may not be necessary to decide which factor is most important; in that case, brainstorming would be sufficient to elicit ideas. If, however, the class needed to determine the most important reasons for Sylvia's decision (or if it wanted to decide on a course of action, in another example), nominal group technique would be helpful.

In using nominal group technique, class members would determine the criteria for voting, after they have completed the brainstorming process. For example, if members of the senior class were discussing the possibilities for a speaker at their graduation, they would list all of their ideas so that everyone could see the entire list. These might include the following:

1. A political figure who will address a current problem
2. Someone from the world of education
3. A speaker who will provide entertainment

4. A school board member
5. Someone who is an alumnus/ae of the school

Before voting on these, the seniors would decide criteria. The speaker's fee, for example, might be important, as well as other factors. These might include the following:

1. Must not charge more than $500
2. Must be available on June 12
3. Must have spoken to other graduation audiences
4. Must have been heard by someone in the class

Then individuals would choose the items from the original brainstorming list that are preferred and that meet the established criteria. The team leader would suggest the number to be selected from the list, say three. Each class member writes each option from the brainstorming list on a separate card, then ranks that option by writing a 3 on the item that he or she most prefers, a 2 on the next-ranked option, and a 1 on the last-choice item. In this way, each class member will have indicated his or her top three choices from the brainstormed list, and will have given a ranking to each.

After votes are recorded (by listing all votes next to the item itself), the group discusses the results openly, in order to identify inconsistent voting patterns (such as items that have received both high and low votes) and to develop a sense of consensus on the approach to be used. If there are members of the class who cannot support the outcome, a final vote can be taken to include other items about which the class felt strongly. After the course of action is determined, team members can brainstorm lists of actual speakers who reflect that course and who meet the selection criteria.

By diminishing the impact of small but vocal members of a group or class, nominal group technique helps to build teamwork while moving toward decisions. Other tools, such as affinity diagrams or the Crawford slip method (see glossary) are also useful in team building, and should be used as appropriate in the team process.

Benefits of team learning

In the brainstorming example using "A White Heron," the process of team evaluation and group discussion evolves, and students find themselves acquiring competencies. These include not only skills with tools and their use, but also deeper understanding of the concepts and analytical skills fundamental to an understanding and appreciation of works of literature. This is likewise true for other disciplines.

Clearly there are times when the tools described here are inappropriate. For example, in learning a mathematical technique, there is information that must be provided as part of the students' learning. Creatively brainstormed responses are not demanded when a group needs to check its answer to a long division problem or to learn the fundamentals of quadratic equations. It is the facilitator's role to assess which tools are most useful in the problem-solving process, not only to solve the problem at hand but also to develop a sense of group responsibility for the solution. Brainstorming supports the discovery approach to learning in math and sciences, encouraging students to consider all the available data and then arriving at the most likely conclusion.

For schools, team learning is earning increased respect. Team learning, as in the example of brainstorming about Jewett's short story, enhances students' ability to see beyond their own viewpoints. In other words, teams learning together are better able to focus on their shared vision than are individuals working to solve the problems separately. A team of thespians rehearsing a drama production is inspired by its vision of the ultimate performance and how each role will contribute to that performance. An individual actor who is rehearsing his or her lines, on the other hand, is operating in a vacuum of inspiration. If, for example, a drama production were rehearsed by having all actors work individually or with only a director to memorize lines, follow blocking directions, and modulate speaking levels, the final production might be flawless in terms of individual performance. It would certainly be a different product, however, from that which has been prepared in group rehearsal with the suggestion, support, and cooperation of other actors.

Individual learning is enhanced in teams, but teams themselves can learn, too. What is known as *synergy* involves the maxim that the sum of the parts of a group is greater than the individual parts. There are examples in the arts, scientific endeavors, and sports, where the intelligence of the team exceeds the intelligence of the individuals on the team and where teams develop extraordinary capacities for coordinated action. Teams that focus on learning together produce exceptional results, with individual members of the teams actually growing more rapidly than they would have with individual effort only (Senge 1990).

Collective learning

When teachers organize students to work in teams, they are not only providing them with structures within which to solve real problems and develop creative solutions, but teachers are also, simultaneously, meeting the needs of their external customers. Managers' top complaint about employees is that so few of them know how to work well with others (Warren 1989). College residence advisors and counsellors observe how difficult it is for entering first-year students to get along with roommates and others in their living areas. Their school experience has been largely an individual one, where they have been rewarded for independence rather than for their contribution to the group, and where rewards have been a source of competition. The individual grade point average is used as a tool to measure success in school. For the role that students will play in their work lives, this measure is not only artificial, but it, in fact, measures the wrong things.

In industry, Deming (1986) emphasizes that teamwork is sorely needed throughout the company. "Teamwork requires one to compensate with his [or her] strength someone else's weakness, for everyone to sharpen each other's wits with questions" (p. 25). Many managers find collective inquiry inherently threatening—perhaps because they have learned in school about the importance of being right. The traditional school experience trains students not to admit that they do not know answers, Deming asserts. The student whose hand is raised first—not the one who mulls an issue over and considers its implications—is often considered to be the star in a classroom. On the other hand, teamwork in an atmosphere of trust builds confidence to take risks and to ask questions. Students who have not been encouraged to take these risks will find it difficult to succeed in this kind of environment in their work lives as well as in their social and family situations.

A cooperatively structured learning situation, as compared to a competitive one, "promotes positive relationships between students and school personnel, positive relationships among students, motivation to do well as students, willingness to get involved in learning activities, positive self-attitudes, and a variety of other affective and cognitive learning outcomes including higher achievement" (Johnson and Algren 1976, 92). But in most schools, children are forced to work against each other, competing for grades and recognition. Although it has been demonstrated that cooperation among students is more supportive of learning, it is competition that is most often emphasized in schools.

A Woburn, Massachusetts, middle school teacher began an experiment in cooperative learning in 1988 that resulted in demonstrated improvement in science and social skills. By working together toward a shared purpose, students improved their performance not only with respect to scientific concepts but also in terms of their ability to work together (Franklin 1990). The same results can be observed in other areas as well; certainly creativity is enhanced in an atmosphere of support and shared vision. The experience of the young women in Vermont demonstrates how they were able to accomplish far more in an atmosphere of trust and cooperation than they might have achieved as individuals who happened to be in a group setting. This is particularly true for those whose self-esteem may have been buffeted by repeated failures in terms of grades and class rewards.

While the ideal of teamwork and cooperation is a positive goal for most classrooms, certain aspects of the system undermine the possibility of fully attaining this ideal. Often, because of teachers' lack of understanding of the benefits of working together, those students who cooperate in their learning are considered cheaters, and are seen as bypassing the system rather than enhancing it. When teachers see students whispering in groups or consulting others for help, they assume only the worst—that the young people are not relying on their own resources but are instead borrowing from others. ("Let's not borrow our neighbor's work," the fifth-grade teacher chants.) Indeed, what may be happening is enhanced understanding derived from the support of another—a validation of one's own thinking, or a challenge to that thinking.

Individuals and interdependence

In a classroom where individual success, rather than teamwork, is emphasized, each student becomes his or her own subsystem, competing with other subsystems for rewards, resources, or attention. The success of one often means the failure of another. That child whose hand is the first to wave in the air with the answer to a teacher's question is often considered a winner, while those who are slower to respond each lose, in some way. Associated with such quick response is a series of positive characteristics, whether they actually apply or not. Examples include quick-wittedness, alertness, attentiveness, or preparation. In fact, the student who ponders, challenges, or pursues an alternative approach is sometimes slower to respond, and does not receive the benefit of the same positive labels. That student instead may be considered slow, unable to concentrate, unwilling to participate, not task-oriented, or a variety of other pejorative terms.

Subtly, the very purpose for being in school has been subverted in this example; the goal becomes not to enhance one's learning, but to be the first to raise one's hand. Imagine a classroom where every student focuses on this goal, to the exclusion of all others. To every question, the response would be a flurry of hand activity. The winner would be defined as the first to be recognized. Since only one student can be first, others would lose, in each day's new competitive game. Of course, in another sense, everyone loses, since the competition militates against thoughtful analysis or creative synthesis, substituting the value of being first for more important learning goals.

When recognition and rewards come with certain behaviors, students are quick to identify the value that teachers place on those behaviors, and students adapt their responses accordingly. When a student races to raise a hand first rather than to develop a careful and thoughtful response, what happens is suboptimization. The act of raising one's hand no longer contributes to the larger purpose of the classroom—that of learning, enhancing understanding, and expressing new ideas—but becomes a process in itself that is subject to enhancement.

What is required is optimization of the entire system, not suboptimization of its individual parts. The example of the child whose hand is raised first presents an illustration of the process of suboptimization. Likewise, a school system that focuses on developing excellent athletics programs, reading skills, or test scores by diverting great proportions of resources to these efforts is also suboptimizing, that is, improving one component of the system rather than enhancing the quality of the entire system as a system. As observed in chapter 2, if a school wanted to demonstrate its excellence in third-grade math, it could devote all of its resources to that program. All teachers would teach only math, and students would spend entire days studying this discipline. With enough attention to math for third graders, certainly that part of the program would improve. But it must be asked whether excellence in one part of the program serves the larger purpose of the school, and whether even that excellence would evaporate as soon as resources are diverted elsewhere.

Single vision and teamwork

When the focus is on optimization of the system as a whole, the need for cooperation and communication becomes clear. The leader/manager's role becomes one of fostering cooperation by focusing on the team's shared vision, rather than of providing knowledge to its members. In music, sports, or other team systems, the larger the number of participants, the greater the demands on the leadership of the teacher/director/coach. Dependence on the orchestra conductor, for example, increases as the size of the group grows. Sheer logistics prevents one section of an orchestra from communicating on an ongoing basis with those on the other side of the room. The section members can get together and discuss problems after the rehearsal, but conversation and in-depth discussion of style cannot take place within the work session. Thus, the dependence on the manager or conductor is critical in providing the vision and facilitating the participation of all members.

The smaller the team, on the other hand, the greater the individual interdependence necessary to achieve quality; that is, the less important is the role of an outside leader or facilitator. A massed choir preparing to sing Handel's *Messiah* requires far more leadership-direction than a small string ensemble, where communication is individual and cooperation is intuitive. A quartet does not require an orchestra conductor for its downbeat. In the rehearsal of a small ensemble, group members frequently communicate with one another, observing and relating how each one's part fits in with the whole. When all members of the group are talented, skilled players, each intuitively understands that his or her success is dependent on the other group members' ability to cooperate. A rehearsal of this group is characterized by repeated playing, stopping, and interacting verbally about the meaning of certain phrases. What ensues is a kind of consensus, with musicians working to discover methods of playing the piece of music well. This self-managed work group is inspired by its members' shared vision of the performance and commitment to cooperative improvement in bringing that vision to reality. But in both cases—that of the small self-managed team as well as the large, complex group—the success of the performance depends on the ability of the individual to contribute in a cooperative way. The leadership skills that are demanded may be different, but the focus on the system as a system is fundamental to success.

No orchestra could function with 100 prima donnas or with individuals bent on being the best they can be regardless of how their performance affects the rest of the group. In other words, when individuals suboptimize by starring with their own performances, they may jeopardize the success of the music produced by the entire orchestra. Paradoxically, being one's best without regard to how his or her individual effort contributes to the success of the whole may actually destroy the group effort—and the outcome—rather than enhancing it. Excellent individual skills do not alone assure outstanding performances, as was seen in the example of a drama production.

The same observations can be made about sports. An 11-person football team is highly dependent on the coaching staff. During a game, plays are often sent in by coaches. Quarterbacks who call their own plays—even in the face of enhanced sophistication and skill levels of these players—are becoming increasingly rare as the game continues to evolve into a complex system. A five-person basketball team, on the other hand, is continually talking while playing, giving verbal and nonverbal signals to the other players, and playing with a high degree of interdependence. For example, teammates will remind one another about remaining time-outs or give signals about defensive maneuvers. Even with only five people on a basketball court, often one person calls the plays and assumes a facilitator role. In both cases, however, the team is committed to team success; individuals are willing to depend on others to bring about this success and to support the efforts of a teammate rather than insisting on starring individual roles. If every member of an

NCAA basketball tournament team capitalized only on individual shooting opportunities rather than working for success of both offense and defense, the team would not be able to optimize its efforts as a team. Interdependence and teamwork assure the success of the effort.

Just as for the members of the ensemble, however, teamwork must be backed by theory and must be supported by problem-solving skills and tools. Individual talent alone does not assure success for the system. Likewise, teamwork alone will not bring about improvement in the system. Each member must have an understanding of the desired outcome and of his or her contribution to success in that outcome. Unless the members have a clear understanding of why they are doing what they are doing, and a vision of their success, the teamwork will fail, or will become only an exercise in social interaction for its members. Students who cannot actively improve the learning situation for themselves will view team exercises as just that—opportunities to get together with classmates, with little other value to the activity.

Team members who come up with good ideas must feel that they can make recommendations that will be considered in a supportive environment. Teamwork must support the purpose of the system, which is to enhance learning. Without support for new ideas, that purpose will be subverted. In a classroom, students love to break into small groups for activities. Without a sense of direction for these activities, the groups become ends in themselves—a kind of suboptimization of the classroom system. When teams are formed with only a vague sense of their purpose, the teacher's role becomes one of police officer, rather than facilitator for learning. Ultimately, teams cooperate with one another to enhance the success of the classroom system. The classroom, related as it is to other learning systems in the school, supports and cooperates with those systems. Interdependence is what characterizes systems and defines the world in which students live.

Giving teams the right to fail

Cooperation takes risk. Someone has to take the first step to begin to work together. The long-term benefits of cooperation are clear, but in the short term, groups that work together may experience frustration, since the team process is time-consuming and demanding. Teachers and administrators—as well as their students—who are not willing to take risks and allow people to work together and to innovate without fear, will never reap the benefits of investing in the improvement of their learning opportunities as team members.

Systems are never fixed or finished; they exist instead in a dynamic world with increasingly complex relationships and interdependencies.

This interrelatedness of systems demands great emphasis on the skills of cooperation and teamwork. The world itself, seen not in the old Newtonian mechanistic view but in the new approach of modern physics, offers a physical basis for a more-integrated and less-fragmented way of seeing ourselves in the world (Zohar 1990) The optimism generated by a world view of interdependence and dynamic growth is reflected in the vision of students working together in common purpose, cooperating for mutual learning, and challenging one another to higher creativity.

In working together to bring about a common purpose, teams must also be given the right to fail. People must know that even if their ideas fall flat they will not be ridiculed or that they will be punished by poor grades or other withholding of rewards. Certainly they cannot be graded on the quality of their contributions to the team activity. It is only with this freedom to fail forward that innovation and genuine creative thinking emerge.

As chapter 7 will suggest, brain theory reinforces the role of cooperation, teamwork, and failure in producing the desired product of the educational system—learning itself. What teachers often know by common sense and accrued experience is supported by what researchers have discovered about the neurology and psychology of the brain and its function in the learning process.

Notes

Ball, M., M. J. Cleary, S. Leddick, C. Schwinn, D. Schwinn, and E. Torres. 1992. *Improvement tools for education (K–12)*. Dayton, Ohio: QIP/PQ Systems.

Deming, W. Edwards. 1986. *Out of the crisis*. Cambridge, Mass.: MIT Center for Advanced Engineering Study.

Franklin, Marie C. 1990. Students gain by working cooperatively. *Boston Globe*, 9 September.

Jewett, Sarah Orne. 1990. A white heron. In *The American tradition in literature*. 7th ed. Vol. 2. Edited by S. G. Perkins, S. Bradley, R. C. Beatty, and E. H. Long. New York: McGraw-Hill.

Johnson, David W., and Andrew Ahlgren. 1976. Relationship between student attitudes about cooperation and competition and attitudes toward schooling. *Journal of Education Psychology* 68, no. 1:92–102.

Kohn, Alfie. 1986. *No contest: The case against competition*. New York: Houghton Mifflin.

Senge, Peter. 1990. *The fifth discipline: The art and practice of the learning organization*. New York: Doubleday.

Senge, Peter, C. Roberts, R. Ross, B. Smith, and A. Kleiner. 1994. *The fifth discipline fieldbook: Strategies and tools for building a learning organization.* New York: CurrencyDoubleday.

Warren, W.J. 1989. Education: New movement seeks to replace rivalry with team spirit. *New York Times,* 4 January.

Zohar, D. 1990. *The quantum self: Human nature and consciousness defined by the new physics.* New York: William Morrow & Company.

Chapter 7

Quality and Learning Theory

Particularly today, when so many difficult and complex problems face the human species, the development of broad and powerful thinking is desperately needed. There should be a way . . . to encourage . . . the intellectual development of . . . youngsters. Instead we find, in the instructional and examination systems of most of these countries, an almost reptilian ritualization of the educational process. I sometimes wonder whether the appeal of sex and aggression in contemporary American television and film offerings reflects the fact that the R-complex is well developed in all of us, while many neocortical functions are, partly because of the repressive nature of schools and societies, more rarely expressed, less familiar, and insufficiently treasured.

—Carl Sagan
The Dragons of Eden

"Although Patrick is bright and creative and contributes actively to class discussions, he cannot stay on task with written work."

"He is not working to his potential, although he is a joy to have in the class because of his eagerness to learn."

"When this student is given leadership opportunities in class, he always shines. But he cannot do the written work that is expected of him, and his grade reflects this."

"His homework is so sloppy that I cannot tell if he has done the work correctly."

"This student always responds accurately when he is asked a question in class, but he does not do well on tests."

"I wish he could get himself organized."

"Patrick must try harder to be neat."

These comments, taken from actual records of progress for a student with difficulty in handwriting, identify a pattern in his work. Bright and capable, he had never had any of his work posted on a teacher's bulletin board as an elementary school student because it was so messy.

111

Even his efforts at creating Mother's Day cards were quickly filed away in his folder by primary-grade teachers who did not want his work exhibited with that of other, neater students.

A natural leader with a sense of humor to compensate for what would have been otherwise a sense of failure, his average grade in high school was a C. On written comments, his teachers unfailingly remarked on his eagerness to learn, his interest in pursuing ideas on his own, his ability to share orally in class, and his inability to write clearly. He was never able to conform to teachers' demands for legible handwriting, carefully drawn pictures, or accurate graphic representations of objects. He had a hard time organizing things in traditional ways. His teachers variously attributed this failure to laziness, lack of interest, immaturity, natural sloppiness, or recalcitrance. "He wants to learn *his* way, not the way of the class," one teacher remarked.

When Patrick was a junior in high school, at the request of his parents and the school counsellor, he was given a computer to take notes and extra time to complete written tests. His grades improved substantially; he was able to demonstrate what he knew in ways that were appropriate to his learning style and particular intelligence. Once he was freed of the mantra "try harder to be neat," his performance blossomed and his natural gifts were recognized for what they were rather than as "yes, buts."

Patterns of learning

This might be considered a classic case study of a so-called learning disabled student whose "disability" was not discovered so that he could be put into special-education classes. Considering it instead as it relates to learning styles and multiple intelligences, a clear learning pattern can be identified. Patrick's pattern fits rather neatly, for example, in Markova's (1992) classification of children's learning styles in terms of three learning approaches and their combinations. A child's conscious mind uses the kinesthetic, auditory, or visual channel; the subconscious mind and the unconscious mind have the same three possibilities.

So a child might be what Markova calls AKV (consciously auditory, subconsciously kinesthetic, unconsciously visual), KAV, VKA, and so on. The diversity that potentially exists among children with respect to their channels of learning, and the amount of variation that will therefore ensue in the classroom experience are readily apparent. The complexity of the mind is accurately suggested in this system of classification. No child can be seen as completely auditory in his or her learning, for example, any more than a student can be seen as totally right brained or left brained, although parents and teachers sometimes mistakenly attribute behavior to this kind of overly simplified classification.

Certainly this kind of research suggests that any single approach to learning will not be appropriate for a classroom of children. Further, a consideration of variation in students' learning channels reinforces the value of working in teams, where each student's own approach will lend richness to the outcome while supporting self-esteem and learning for all members of the team.

Our student Patrick had indeed learned a great deal during his elementary and high school years. An independent learner, he excelled in situations where there were no limits to his performance rather than in the classroom with its teacher-created bounds. He was a standout in small-group projects and discussions, in nontraditional assignments such as parodies or video projects.

But his particular learning style was not one that was recognized as valid in his school setting. Teachers would sometimes refuse to give oral tests because they did not consider it "fair to other students" to give him this attention. Some would not extend a testing period for him: "If he can't learn to take a test in 50 minutes, he'll never make it in college."

As we learn more about intelligence and its many manifestations, as well as the variety of learning styles that young people demonstrate, it becomes clear that student performance cannot be considered only as it relates to traditional, structured, written-work-only assignments. Such structure, when it is externally imposed without regard to the larger context of learning, is severely limiting to a child's possibilities. Authentic learning reflects an understanding of connecting concepts to students' experiences. For example, rather than memorizing a list of computer terms, learning how a computer works can be done by examining its parts or using it for a complex task. Also, rather than learning for a test, learning for an application may be appropriate. In addition to content that is learned from application, the immediate feedback from such learning includes *metacognition,* or knowing what one knows. Knowing the tools for laboratory analysis of a dissected frog well enough to apply them in a new situation, such as in dissecting a fetal pig, assures users about their level of competence with such tools. Merely taking a test that requires students to memorize the tools and their definitions assures learners of nothing, except perhaps their ability to do that task in isolation from any application.

From Gardner's (1983) articulation of a variety of "intelligences," it is clear that students learn best not only logically, but also kinesthetically, spatially, rhythmically, linguistically, intrapersonally and interpersonally. Each of the intelligences that Gardner identifies has a concomitant description of neurological process, capacities, and developmental journey.

Individual students' differences lie in the balance and combinations of these intelligences (Gardner 1991).

Connections for learning

From other research, what has been learned about the brain suggests that it is, in fact, connections that empower learning. When students are able to connect new knowledge in a meaningful way with past experience, it is learned. When no such connection occurs, it may be memorized for some extrinsic, short-term reward, but no real learning ensues (Caine and Caine 1991). The classroom experience may be seen as an upward gyre or spiral, where students return to what has been already learned, but see it in light of new applications or meanings. A poem to very young children might be represented in a simple, sing-songy rhyme. Each new exposure to poetry builds on that original concept and expands its sophistication. Fifth graders can read *Huckleberry Finn* and enjoy its sense of adventure and freedom. High school juniors can once again experience Twain's novel, bringing enhanced insight, new understandings of freedom, and an appreciation for language. The connection between the two readings is fundamental to the expanded, enriched experience.

Quality learning enhances teachers' abilities to support and encourage students regardless of their learning styles or particular intelligences, because it helps teachers facilitate learning rather than impart it. This is another manifestation of quality learning's emphasis on "doing with" rather than "doing to" students.

One of the paradoxes of educational systems is that they are often among the least likely organizations to provide for ongoing learning for their teachers. Professional organizations for teachers, struggling with issues of compensation and working conditions, sometimes fail to bring new life to their members' professional development. While a certain number of courses may be required to assure continued certification, these courses often have little to do with what the teacher actually does in the day-to-day school environment, working with actual students. Indeed, teachers may take courses for future positions, focusing not on improvement of the classroom but instead on hoped-for promotions to administrative or counselling positions. Annual educational conferences help, but teachers often find these to be either irrelevant to their teaching situation or so specific to another classroom environment that they are of little use in developing new understandings about students and their learning. And after reaching a certain point in the certification process, teachers may no longer be expected to engage in ongoing professional development activities at all.

On the other hand, those in other professions often expect opportunities for learning to be an ongoing part of their work life. In recent years, for example, businesses have invested millions of dollars in ongoing training for their staffs—everything from using a specific software program to learning how to supervise others and how to deal with difficult colleagues. One large electronics firm spends $200 million per year on teaching skills to employees. Surgeons, hearing about new procedures, pursue various avenues of learning in which they can bring themselves up to date on the best approaches to their own specialties. Staying current is one of the challenges that physicians take most seriously, according to the president of an Ohio medical society—which is an organization that, like education organizations, deals with political issues and work life, but also spends a great deal of effort in educating physicians about developments in the profession that will improve the practice of medicine.

This void in opportunities for educators' professional development is significant, because it often means that teachers miss opportunities to understand current thinking that may revolutionize the way in which students are taught. For example, although teachers may be aware of research on how the brain functions in the learning process, many have not studied brain theory since undergraduate days, and many have no knowledge of cutting-edge breakthroughs about brain theory in learning. The neurosciences have much to offer that will help educators fully understand their roles, but the fact is that teachers have few formal opportunities to garner support from this source. (Likewise, those in the neurosciences often fail to tap into teachers' immense knowledge about students in order to enrich their research. A dialogue between the scientific community and the educational community would surely benefit both.)

Brain research and classroom implications

Those familiar with research in this area are taking advantage of the brain's capacity to learn. Without this familiarity, educators will continue to go about organizing classrooms, schedules, and teaching in the same ways they have always done. And, as we have noted, schools will continue to get what they are getting if they keep doing what they have always done. New ways of working together make it possible to help students to take on increasingly complex intellectual challenges with greater levels of creativity and confidence than previously thought to be possible. By understanding learning theory, educators can expand schools' ability to support young people's native ability to grow and develop in a learning environment. Understanding what is developmentally appropriate for a child at a given age also supports the learning process (Elkind 1981).

The learning environment that is most fundamental to the school experience is the classroom itself, where applications of research about learning have genuine implications for the ways that learning is best facilitated. Renate Nummela Caine and Geoffrey Caine (1991) point out that much of the "new" educational theory and methods have been done or said before, but that what is needed is a new "framework" that will enable educators to make use of what they already know. That framework, they suggest, must integrate human behavior and perception as well as emotions and physiology. This is the framework for what has become known as brain-based learning, which involves "acknowledging the brain's rules for meaningful learning, and organizing teaching with those rules in mind" (p. 4).

When educators assume that most learning takes place through information that is imparted by teachers and memorized for application later, they are ignoring a great deal about how the learning process actually works. The human mind learns by connecting the new with the old, or by recognizing and naming experiences that may already be well known. Children who see rectangles from an early age, for example, will eventually be told in school the definition of a rectangle by a math teacher, who assumes no prior knowledge of rectangles but instead defines the term for students. It is sometimes assumed that the many years' experience with rectangles that children may accumulate has nothing to do with learning, which can be imparted only by a teacher in a classroom.

A not-yet-three-year-old, picnicking with his parents and an older friend in a park, sees a gate leading to an adjoining field. Pointing to the gate, he yells excitedly, "H! H!"

Puzzled, his parents look at the gate. "No, Sean. Gate."

"H! H!" he continues to yell, becoming frustrated with his parents' inability to understand him.

After several minutes Sean breaks into frustrated tears, leaving his baffled parents shaking their heads and looking intently at the fence, the gate, and the cows beyond to try to guess what he is trying to identify. It is only when Sean's older friend returns from the playground that the puzzle is solved.

"Oh—he sees the *H* on the fence," she patiently explains. The shape of the crossbars and upright supports indeed makes the shape of an *H,* at least to someone who has just learned to recognize the shape of the letter in a picture book, and is alert to its appearance. Sean's parents' concern is quickly transformed into amazement at the brilliance of their small child.

Like these baffled parents, teachers are often unable to capitalize on their students' established experiences to build knowledge. They themselves have been trained to do well with academic learning, with its emphasis on memorization outside of meaningful experience, so they are unable to see the *H*s in their students' lives.

Orchestrating connections

Learning, however, can take place only when these connections are actually made. Teachers facilitate connections, or orchestrate the learning that goes on in students' brains, establishing appropriate environments, materials, technology, and support to assure that the learning will take place, and developing a context for learning.

Distinguishing between route (or taxon) learning and map learning, brain research suggests that specific, concrete information is important, but it is most successfully introduced into students' experiences by using this information to build understanding. Returning to the language of Alfred North Whitehead (1929) introduced in chapter 5, the learning process can be seen in terms of its development from "romance," or the enthusiasm that comes from discovery of a new idea or experience, through "precision," to "generalization." The first two stages are essential, North asserts, to the third, for what he calls "precision" entails understanding concrete application, formal language, and detailed information about new ideas. By moving from the first to the second stage, students are able to finally come to an ability to generalize about their experiences with some degree of accuracy. If the early stages are skipped, the ability to generalize is impaired because it has no basis in love of learning or in fact.

Other educational philosophers identify stages in learning as well; the developmental aspects of the learning process are clearly documented. Sometimes teachers and parents substitute information (precision, taxon learning, and so on) for the larger experience of knowledge acquisition. An example of a classroom experience will be familiar to many high school students.

The lesson relates to literary terms and figures of speech—those peculiar devices that poets and other weird writers use to avoid getting down to brass tacks, according to one high school sophomore. For teachers pressed by the constraints of a 50-minute class period and a 10-week term, the most efficient way to teach these devils seems to be to make a list, have learners look up definitions, go over these in class, and then have a test on them. Teachers smile smugly as they walk down the hall on test day and overhear students frantically asking each other,

"What's the difference between a simile and a metaphor?" or "What do you have for hy-per-BOLE?" The pretest frenzy seems to offer bizarre reinforcement that the system works.

And, in fact, it may seem to when the teachers look at the tests. With only a slight confusion between metonymy and synecdoche, most students seem to have mastered the list. Of course, that is the point: Young learners can indeed master lists of information when pressed by exigency to do so. But understanding how this fits into a love of poetry and its sound—something that might be established before demanding memorization of any kind of list—or using it to apply to other areas in their lives, will be impossible when the list exists in a kind of vacuum.

If the motivation for learning were to be examined, it is clear that in this exercise students will learn the list because of the test—extrinsic motivation at its most basic. With respect to brain activity, a relatively small number of neurons is firing repeatedly in memorization—a process that results in quick fatigue and the need for frequent rests. The job is not likely to be stimulating, unless it becomes part of a larger pattern that depends on intrinsic motivation (Caine and Caine 1991).

Making it stick

Teachers who have had the interesting experience of teaching the same group of learners two years in a row know the likelihood that this group of students will remember the list of literary terms and their definitions well enough to explain them the following year. This phenomenon is what makes teachers roll their eyes toward heaven and ask themselves why they stay in the profession. Sometimes, nothing seems to stick.

If, however, the acquisition of knowledge is rooted in the learners' experiences, it will stay with them with each new application of it. How can teachers make this connection with their students?

Approaches would, of course, be different for younger children than for high school learners, but look at some examples. Third-grade teachers, reinforcing their students' learning about apples, meet to plan ways in which various experiences could facilitate this learning. After this planning, the librarian reads stories about apples, and the science teacher gives each children apple sections cut both crosswise and segmented so they can see the inside of the fruit. A parent who collects antique tools brings in an apple cider press and the children make cider, noting the taste and smell of the juice. During their art class, students make dolls with apple faces that dry into amusing caricatures. Children draw apples, write stories about apples, bring in different varieties of apples to share, and do library reports about apples. They are introduced to the legendary Johnny Appleseed and write their own tall tales and songs, which they share with their classmates. A field trip to an apple farm includes a wagon ride through the orchard and a chance to pick apples.

Notice that these approaches not only reinforce children's eagerness to experience and learn, but also touch their multiple intelligences as well. These include the following:

- Logical, mathematical: scientifically measuring the apple, counting the seeds, and using encyclopedias to research the apple
- Interpersonal: sharing discussions about apples and working together on apple dolls and cider making
- Intrapersonal: creative writing about experiences and feelings associated with apples and identifying fictional characters' motivations
- Musical/rhythmic: singing and using percussive instruments to create music centered on the theme of apples
- Verbal/linguistic: explaining, reporting, and telling stories about apples
- Visual/spatial: seeing and feeling apples in a lab, drawing and visiting the orchard
- Body/kinesthetic: touching, smelling, tasting, and picking apples

An elementary school approach might offer a variety of experiences such as those listed, or it could revolve around learning stations where young people choose activities that suit their own styles. A high school lesson may be more sophisticated, but it, too, can reach young people's interest, experience, and learning styles, and offer them choices about how to learn. By developing students' need for choices in their learning, an interdisciplinary experience might look like the following:

An advanced Spanish class is reading a Cervantes novel. As students develop ways to demonstrate their understanding of the language as well as fundamental elements of theme, plot, character, and setting in the novel, they can brainstorm a variety of activities that will do just that. A teacher, as knowledge facilitator, may encourage them to expand their list to reach all types of intelligences. The list from which students can choose for their own approaches might include the following:

- Make a three-dimensional model of a setting from the novel (kinesthetic)
- Invent a board game relating to the theme of the novel (visual)
- Make a calendar or timetable of events (logical/mathematical)
- Write an additional chapter to the novel (linguistic)

- Assemble a costume for a character in the book (visual, kinesthetic)
- Create musical accompaniment for a scene in the novel (musical/rhythmic)
- Use an overhead projector and transparencies to present a character analysis, hypothesis about the novel's structure, and so on. (logical, visual)
- Dramatize a scene or chapter from the book (kinesthetic)
- Categorize facts about characters (logical/mathematical)
- Create a journal as if you were Don Quixote (intrapersonal)
- Create dialogue about the book (in Spanish) and perform with a classmate (interpersonal)
- Create a poem about an aspect of the novel (linguistic)

Choices: Learning how to learn best

Offering choices such as these not only provides a variety of approaches to learning styles, but also offers choices for students to make about their learning. Nine-year-old Kendra observed, "I really learn best when I get to help plan how I'm going to learn." For students to take responsibility for their own learning, it is important for them to examine the learning process itself, so that they can evaluate for themselves not only what they are learning, but how they are learning, and how they know that they are learning. Knowledge about the process (subsystem) improves the process itself as well as its outcomes. Of course, this is consistent with systems thinking, for in identifying systems of learning, students can also focus on the purpose of those systems.

A highly effective way to provide opportunities for students to reinforce their learning and create connections with their earlier-learned experiences is through a cross-disciplinary approach. Students might learn a great deal about ancient Greece, for example, by creating a mock Olympics program. They might find themselves pursuing research about the original games and about their origins in Greece before they stage the event, not only performing long jumps but also measuring and calculating them. Applications of skills in writing, speaking, and measuring, as well as concepts from physics, language study (both Greek and English), history, economics, and political science abound as students go about creating this event.

Returning to the systems approach to education, in order for these kinds of learning opportunities to take place, the class scheduling system must be examined, and perhaps altered. The disciplines for thinking are not the same as the ways in which young people's days are organized. Further, the daily 50-minute class periods, for example, might militate against students' ability to fully pursue their learning. This observation may reflect practical realities—the Olympic games could never be enacted within the constraints of a single class period. And yet, as John Dewey acknowledged long ago, firsthand contact with physical actualities is essential to learning. To Dewey, experience *is* education. Certainly the best aspects of his thinking apply to the interdisciplinary opportunities that schools provide for students today. When administrative concerns such as scheduling interfere with rather than support these processes, there can be no constancy of purpose in the learning system.

The venerable generalist Alfred North Whitehead (1929), too, called for schools to eradicate the disconnection of subjects which "kills the vitality of our modern curriculum" (p. 10). Whitehead called the subject breakup reflected in high schools "a rapid table of contents" that someone might review while thinking of a way to create something before figuring out how to give it order.

Another reason that rigidly scheduled slots for classes may militate against genuine learning lies in the concept of "flow" as it is understood by psychologists such as Mihaly Csikszentmihalyi (1990). Optimal learning experience, Csikszentmihalyi says, occurs when one is so immersed in a meaningful activity—work or leisure—that concentration is not interrupted by any sense of time's passage, the need for food, or other distractions. A sense of purpose, enjoyment, and order carry learners through a sense of unity and involvement with the work at hand. People who become lost in reading, writing, computer programming, or drawing, as well as those who pursue intense physical activities such as rock climbing or marathon swimming know this experience, and recognize the joy in the activity that it represents. When learners organize work tasks in such a way as to frequently bring about this experience, their quality of life is indeed enhanced, Csikszentmihalyi asserts.

Rather than contributing to the possibility of this kind of in-depth concentration, the pinball-machine schedule of most schools precludes its occurrence from happening entirely. Learning is segmented and fragmented, so that students who really get into an idea must quickly abandon the possibility of pursuing it with every resource of their minds and imaginations. Before this can happen, the bell will ring to signal that a class period has ended. Students can never learn to become so engrossed in ideas, tasks, or the learning process itself that they experience this deeply rewarding and enjoyable opportunity, when their school experience creates multiple fragmentations of learning and militates against opportunities for connections among learned units.

Teachers, too, are denied the possibility of this intense learning experience, for their days are chopped up by arbitrary schedules. Work space is often limited to common faculty room offices shared with others and replete with the interruption of meetings, student needs, and—of course—class bells. No wonder teachers are so exhausted when they go home; they have not had the refreshment of deep thought or creativity in a flow experience, nor the possibility of quiet insight about what they teach. Here, too, is the connection that quality learning can make between theory and practice. If a school system (including its financial supporters, the taxpayers) sees the value of this kind of experience for teachers because it will contribute to their ability to enhance the purpose of the school itself, the managers of the system will find ways to bring it about.

The concepts of quality learning do not contradict, but indeed support, educators' approaches to harnessing what they know about learning theory and the brain. This is why quality learning cannot be seen as simply another program, operating separately from other school programs. It is instead a way of seeing and understanding, so that the best of other programs and approaches might be utilized to bring about the best that is possible from all learners in the classroom.

What is also clear from this illustration is that total quality, though its practice may have originated in the business community, is not simply a business program template to be imposed on schools. True, the language of customer orientation, as has been seen, comes directly from the world of commerce; but its concept—that of understanding the benefit that accrues to someone who receives what the system has to offer—is fundamentally recognizable to educators. Certainly, understanding what the neurosciences have to say about the brain and the learning process is fundamental to determining the needs of those who receive the benefits of the educational system.

Immersion and learning

Immersion, considered by many to be the most effective way to accommodate learning styles and diversity of intelligences, provides an opportunity to utilize many of the problem-solving and statistical tools that are components of quality learning. For while the concept of immersion has its appeal, learners and their facilitators find that the experience must be carefully structured and planned, if it is not to end in disappointing outcomes and chaotic practices. In other words, simply immersing oneself in an experience, without a clear sense of purpose and desired outcomes, can end up as only a social experience.

A group of learners whose aim is to improve their French language, for example, cannot simply decide to speak only French for a given time. Instead, they must understand how a variety of experiences will support that purpose. When students decide to live in international dorms on university campuses, they may all have their own unrelated purposes in mind. Some of these will relate to language improvement, of course. Others will have more to do with meeting students from other countries, being in a dorm that is more convenient, or following a friend's initiative. If they are not committed to a sense of purpose for their learning, they will find it difficult and even meaningless to ask—in French—a roommate for change for the laundry.

Determining the purpose of the system, assessing ways in which it currently operates, deciding the ways in which it can better serve the purpose of a given group of students, evaluating data suggesting how this is happening, and taking action to assure that the experience will continue to become better are aspects of the total quality cycle that will reinforce this immersion as an effective learning opportunity. Understanding variation will help these students determine whether the system is stable in terms of predetermined measures of its quality.

Taking charge of learning

Of course the tools of quality improvement are useful, even by themselves, in a variety of educational settings. Teachers already use the best aspects of brainstorming, nominal group technique, and even Pareto diagrams or cause-and-effect charts. But how much more powerful these tools are when they are undergirded by that way of seeing and thinking that characterizes quality learning.

Another way of examining the brain and how it functions with respect to learning lies in the physiology of the brain itself. For example, Paul MacLean's (1978, 308–342) "triune brain theory" suggests that the human brain is actually three brains in one. He observes that the development of young people who are motivated by compassion, concern for the future, the ability to look ahead, and other higher-order motivations requires greater use of the prefrontal lobes, the most recent addition to the human brain.

The triune brain theory suggests that the layers of the brain developed in an evolutionary way. The brain's most primitive part, the R-complex, was the earliest to develop in human beings, followed later in the evolutionary process by the limbic system, and the neocortex. While MacLean's is not the first tripartite theory of brain development, it provides a way of looking at the brain in terms of the ways in which young people grow and learn.

The purpose of the R-complex is related to physical survival, fight-or-flight reflexes, and body maintenance. Its manifestations lie in ritualistic and flocking behaviors. The limbic system, on the other hand, houses emotions and serves to inhibit some of the habitual ways of responding that are represented in the R-complex. The thinking brain or neocortex is the center of logical thinking and planning for the future, and is responsible for creating the language of speech and writing. All three layers of the brain interconnect—they do not represent separate behaviors. Instead, they can be acknowledged in the educational process and appealed to in positive ways.

Furthermore, as Caine and Caine (1991, 61) assert, the old brain propensities can be reprogrammed and redirected. "We have at our disposal the capacity to totally rethink what it means to survive and to implement the solutions." What an opportunity this presents to classroom teachers, school administrators, and boards of education. Instead of building on students' violent, physical natures, schools can integrate long-term thinking and survival within the learning process, appealing to and developing the newer layers of the brain by facilitating appropriate learning experiences.

An example of teaching that does this might lie in a comparative approach to violence in literature or film. Showing a movie that is replete with gratuitous violence might stimulate the R-complex, building on young people's primitive and physical sensibilities and generating lively discussion about how the violence was perpetrated or its effect on viewers. On the other hand, seeing a violent film in the context of higher motivations—a documentary about the Holocaust that shows abhorrent, violent acts and human suffering not for their own sake but within the context of heroism, compassion, and justice—may capitalize on the propensities of the primitive brain by connecting it to the best of the neocortex's tendencies.

Mihaly Csikszentmihalyi (1990) describes the function of the brain's consciousness, as distinguished from its unconscious states, to represent information about what is happening both internally and externally so that people can act on that information. In this way, the brain serves as a clearinghouse for all the perceptions, feelings, sensations, and ideas that are experienced, so that a person does not react merely in a reflexive or instinctive way, but can weigh information against past experience or imagination and respond accordingly. This capacity is, in a way, outside of original human genetic tendencies, since it enables people to make themselves happy or unhappy by changing what is in their consciousness, regardless of what is going on in their physical worlds. This ability can be developed, since the mind's untapped potential is so extraordinary. The purpose of education, both formal and informal, might be seen in terms of developing this consciousness, so that human beings function at a higher level than that represented only in instinct or physical responses. The implications for learning are very real.

Language and learning

Psychologist Jane Healy (1990) makes a compelling argument about the place of language acquisition in learning, asserting that learning to speak accurately and precisely actually contributes to the development of learning, rather than merely reflecting this development. If, as in Healy's example, a person has the capacity to describe the color of a geranium with a variety of words (*cerise, scarlet, salmon, red, orange,* and so on) rather than only one—maybe *red*—that capacity actually helps one to think about the color of the geranium. This includes the ability to discriminate among color possibilities, an important thinking skill. Likewise, when children learn fundamental relationships of words within sentences, they are learning about the relationship of ideas. "It is raining," and "I need an umbrella," for example, represent two ideas. When someone says, "Because it is raining, I need an umbrella," a relationship has been established between the two ideas. Expressing the relationship in language helps young people to understand that relationship and to generalize about how to use the cause-effect relationship in other ways, thus expanding their thinking skills and ability to communicate. When young people communicate by saying "You know . . . like . . . he goes . . . I go . . . you know . . . like" and so on, they are demonstrating not only their inability to express their thinking in words, but flaws in their very thinking as well.

Schools can ameliorate flaws in thinking skills when they insist on clear speaking and writing, facilitate vocabulary enrichment through meaningful dialogue and challenging reading, and model clear conversational exchanges. To be sure, educators may do this naturally, if they value clear communication themselves. When educators understand the importance of language development in terms of the learning process itself, however, basing their behaviors on sound theories of brain development, there will be a greater commitment to framing classroom teaching to reflect the larger purpose of the school system with respect to learning. Once again, understanding the "so what" of what we do gives life to behaviors and perspective to practices.

Plateaus of learning

Biophysicist Herman Epstein's (1978, 343–370) analysis of developmental plateaus in brain growth have equally important implications for schools. His research suggests that the brain grows throughout childhood in a series of spurts. During these periods of activity, children are most receptive to learning. The myelin and dendritic connections are actually increasing, he says, in order to form new channels for thinking. Epstein asserts that the brain is at its most teachable during these periods of growth. Between the spurts, the brain experiences a kind of plateau, when it is less receptive to certain kinds of learning.

Periods of rapid physical growth such as that which occurs during middle school years, may not be the best time for heavy emphasis on so-called academic learning, if Epstein's theory is considered. As a middle school teacher in an Ohio school comments about young adolescents, "Prepubescents don't belong in classrooms; they should all be out in fields exercising their muscles." While this open-field model might be difficult to sell to school supporters, the classroom itself can become an appropriate place for these students with an understanding of their developmental needs. Instead, parents often push their children into higher levels of academic content at this age, forcing schools to provide increasingly challenging classroom experiences that may be totally inappropriate to their development and undermining to their long-term learning potential.

In any case, since children do not all experience spurts and plateaus at the same time, the importance of opportunities for children to learn what they are, at that moment, capable of learning, is clear. And punishing children who are not developmentally ready for a particular kind of abstract thinking with low grades can destroy those children's confidence in their ability to learn. Understanding a variety of theories of brain development and learning capacities will reinforce what to many educators is intuitive. It will also give them a sense of the larger system of learning within which their own interactions with children fall.

Of course not one, but many theories about learning and cognitive development have been posited, from the earliest philosophers and thinkers. Plato, after all, believed that all knowledge is inherent, though not remembered, and that the teachers' role was to help students remember or recognize the knowledge within. (Maybe this is why Socrates didn't give gold stars.) This nativist view emerged again in the 1980s, with a focus on development or the maturation process as an unfolding of cognitive development. Modularity hypotheses, the long-standing nature-or-nurture discussion, Piaget's (1969) voice of the 1970s, Heinz Werner's (Werner and Kaplan 1963) organismic-developmental point of view, and others have all given richness to the discussion of cognitive development. Far too many approaches to cognitive development, the brain, and learning have been articulated to be included here. Suffice it to say, that unless educators are operating within the framework of theories upon which they can agree, their attempts to improve their systems will eventually founder.

Techniques for learning

Current theory about cognitive development has been influenced by the computer. In fact, Gardner (1983) calls it the "biggest influence on cognitive development today" not only because of its utility in running experiments and analyzing data, but also because of the model it provides of how children learn and think. Connections between technology and learning have yet to be studied at length, but in their own classroom experiences, teachers see children's excitement in making connections on the computer or creating images with video equipment. Some assert that this phenomenon occurs because young people have been barraged with the auditory and visual stimuli of mass communications media from an early age, and have come to expect these stimuli in their classroom experiences. It may, in fact, develop because such experiences appeal to a variety of approaches to learning. The kinesthetic, the visual, and the auditory opportunities are immediately apparent in the use of computers, for example. These are supplemented by the logical-mathematical, musical, or other specific experiences provided in the actual task in which children are involved.

A technique that is often used by writing teachers demonstrates not only how concepts of quality learning are reflected in established classroom techniques but also how they help teachers use these techniques appropriately and effectively to support learning. In this exercise, students identify general topics about which they want to write. (Quality learning would suggest that the purpose of the writing is clear at the outset.) Once students are engaged in the writing, they record their topics, and then create a kind of spiderweb of related ideas or subsets of the general idea, connecting these ideas in expanding circles. Thinking about the writing process enhances the learning opportunity.

By focusing on a single idea, students are able to capitalize on their own learning styles; develop intrinsic motivation by writing about something in which they have ownership; open the doors to investigation from a variety of their own sources of experience—other reading, observations, and their own lives; utilize tools of brainstorming and affinity diagrams as well as the spider diagram with which they begin; and develop enthusiasm for their writing because they have invested so much in the planning of it. Their motivation will be enhanced when they are given opportunities to determine their own sources and even their own due dates. The quality of the writing will improve if they continue to rewrite it or revise it until it satisfies their own standards of quality writing.

By contrast, frequently a writing experience begins as an assigned topic with a due date, and students find themselves scrambling to determine what is expected—that is, what ideas will be acceptable—rather than focusing on their own leadership of the process. Ideally, the opportunity for the writing experience will come from other experiences: perhaps a visit to an archeological site, or an opportunity to hear a speaker or a poem that students have discovered. In this way, the writing is not an end in itself, but is part of the larger learning experience that is stimulated by the original event.

In this exercise, quality learning theory and tools are demonstrated in the ways in which students approach the writing. At the same time, concepts from learning theory, such as the value of integrating experiences from other disciplines or experiences, are recognized. Jerome Bruner (1959) calls this ability to apply knowledge in new ways "generic learning." If the principle of addition, for example, is grasped at this deep level, it is unnecessary to "learn" multiplication, since multiplication is, in principle, only repeated addition. These mathematical processes have key relationships to one another. Instead, they are often treated as separate units in the curriculum.

Learning and the purpose of education

Understanding learning theory undoubtedly supports educators' ability to define the purpose of education—a key ingredient to creating quality learning in schools. Knowing how the brain functions with respect to learning also contributes to the inputs of the learning process: selecting the appropriate tools and methodologies; determining how children will be grouped in their learning experiences; and developing strategies to emphasize the intrinsic rewards of learning rather than extrinsic motivation. Neuroscience, neuroanatomy, cognitive science, psychoanalysis, psychology, and artificial intelligence study provide perspectives from which to view the learning process. Educators who understand learning from the vantage point of the schools could derive benefit from these sciences, just as the sciences themselves can gain from the understandings of classroom teachers and school counsellors.

Insights about learning suggest something about teaching. Knowledge of actions and skills is different from knowledge of concepts, for example, and the concomitant teaching-learning activities are appropriately different. Knowing what one knows (metaknowledge) supports the acquisition of new knowledge, creating a capacity for connections to prior knowledge. The implications of learning theory for the classroom are clear enough. It has been suggested that there is "brain-antagonistic" education as well as brain-compatible learning (Hart 1983). When the understanding of learning theory is put into the framework of quality learning, these implications are even more lucid, providing the theoretical framework for understanding the purpose of the school (and of every classroom activity), appreciating variation among students with respect to their rate and depth of learning potential at different stages of development, and clarifying the needs of customers.

For a reality check of the implications of brain and learning theory for the classroom, educators need only to turn to students, who concur in their teachers' understanding of learning theory. Students prefer active learning environments, rather than rigid and passive classrooms. While the ultimate indictment of a classroom is that penetrating judgment—"boring"—students are quick to respond to teachers' efforts to create meaningful frameworks for learning rather than isolated exercises in memorization or information transfer. In classes that are predominantly lecture rather than interactive discussion, students recognize that education is being "done to" them rather than being done with their participation and understanding (Phelan, Davidson, and Cao 1992). This leads to a discussion of leadership, not only in the classroom system, but also in the organization as a whole. A leadership approach that encourages learning, and supports opportunities for teachers and students to make choices about their own learning, is fundamental to the success of the school, just as it is to the success of the individual classroom.

Continuing to define the elephant, quality learning is not neuroscience or psychology, nor is it a specific theory of cognitive development. But quality learning facilitates the application of knowledge from these important studies to the learning process in the classroom, and optimizes that application. Perhaps it can be said that the learning sciences represent the view from the top of the elephant.

Notes

Bruner, Jerome S. 1959. Learning and thinking. *Harvard Educational Review* (summer): 3. Reprinted in *Teachers and the learning process*, edited by Robert D. Strom. 1971. Englewood Cliffs, N.J.: Prentice Hall.

Caine, Renate Nummela, and Geoffrey Caine. 1991. *Making connections: Teaching and the human brain*. Alexandria, Va.: Association for Supervision and Curriculum Development.

Csikszentmihalyi, Mihaly. 1990. *Flow: Psychology of optimal experience*. New York: Harper & Row.

Elkind, D. 1981. *The hurried child: Growing up too fast, too soon*. Reading, Mass.: Addison-Wesley. Elkind offers a provocative discussion of the ways in which society pushes children ahead to physical, intellectual, and social challenges that are often inappropriate to their development.

Epstein, Herman T. 1978. Growth spurts during brain development: Implications for educational policy and practice. In *The 77th yearbook of the national society for the study of education*. Chicago: National Society for the Study of Education. Distributed by University of Chicago Press.

Gardner, Howard. 1983. *Frames of mind: The theory of multiple intelligences*. New York: Basic Books.

———. 1991. *The unschooled mind: How children think and how schools should teach.* New York: Basic Books.

Hart, Leslie. 1983. *Human brain, human learning.* New York: Longman.

Healy, Jane. 1990. *Endangered minds: Why children don't think and what we can do about it.* New York: Touchtone Book/Simon & Schuster.

MacLean, P.D. 1978. A mind of three minds: Educating the triune brain. In *The 77th Yearbook of the national society for the study of education.* Chicago: National Society for the Study of Education. Distributed by University of Chicago Press.

Markova, D. 1992. *How your child is smart: A life-changing approach to learning.* Berkeley, Calif.: Conari Press.

Phelan, P., A. L. Davidson, and H. T. Cao. 1992. Speaking up: Students' perspectives on school. *Phi Delta Kappan,* 73, no 9:695–704. This study also asserts a powerful connection between classroom strategies of teamwork, cooperative learning, and detracking with the potential for breaking down barriers among student groups (racial, social, economic) in school.

Piaget, J. 1969. *The psychology of intelligence.* Translated by M. Piercy and D. E. Berlyne. Totowa, N.Y.: Littlefield, Adams, and Company.

Sagan, Carl. 1977. *The dragons of Eden: Speculations on the evolution of human intelligence.* New York: Random House.

Werner, Heinz, and B. Kaplan. 1963. *Symbol formation: An organismic-developmental approach to language and the expression of thought.* New York: Wiley.

Whitehead, Alfred North. 1929. *The aims of education and other essays.* New York: Macmillan.

Chapter 8

Leadership for Quality

> *I believe that we have only just begun the process of discovering and inventing the new organizational forms that will inhabit the twenty-first century. To be responsible inventors and discoverers, though, we need the courage to let go of the old world, to relinquish most of what we have cherished, to abandon our interpretations about what does and doesn't work. As Einstein is often quoted as saying: No problem can be solved from the same consciousness that created it. We must learn to see the world anew.*
>
> —Margaret J. Wheatley
> *Leadership and the New Science: Learning about Organizations from an Orderly Universe*

A participant at a quality learning seminar asked, "But if top managers allow their employees to make decisions, where does the accountability lie?" He cited a hypothetical example of workers who are empowered to decide their own vacation schedules, and they all pick the same week to take off.

In organizations where the real accountability is to customers and where a sense of purpose, clear systems thinking, understanding of variation, and an awareness of the psychology of human behavior prevail, something like this will not happen. Instead, every member of the organization understands that taking vacations all at once means that customers cannot be served and that the company's mission or purpose is diminished. Group processes and team problem-solving skills help employees determine an acceptable vacation schedule to serve their needs as well as those of the organization and its customers.

It would appear, then, that the role of leadership in any organization, including schools, is to hold all of this together: to assure that all members see the organization as their own, understand the meaning of systems, and clearly identify with the aim of the system. While traditional organizations' structure emphasizes power, it is interdependence that is the hallmark of a total quality organization. When people are ac-

131

tively involved in interdependent efforts characterized by shared vision, the organization will not only produce quality work, but it will also provide opportunities for its members to find joy and meaning in that work.

Relationships that are based on power doom improvement efforts, and are to blame for the "predictable failure of educational reform" that Sarason (1990) notes. That is, when relationships among teachers, administrators, students, and parents are based on a hierarchical, competitive understanding of respective roles, a sense of ownership for the improvement of the organization cannot thrive. For example, a principal invites a team to improve the college counselling process. The group meets throughout the summer, without compensation, as its members invest their energy, enthusiasm, and creativity in the desired outcome. After the process is finished, however, the principal, in announcing the changes that the team has recommended, uses the pronoun *I* rather than *we*. "I've decided to send college counsellors to workshops." "I've made some changes in staffing." "I'm interested in improving our college placements." With that single lapse, the principal demonstrated his interest in his own aggrandizement rather than the good of the organization. (It is doubtful that these team members will so willingly give their energy the next time they are asked.) Rather than power, the basis of leadership and improvement must be built on a sense of vision and a spirit of cooperation.

Speaking louder than words

Leadership, it must be emphasized, is more than words. Those who try to lead with words alone are in precipitous danger of hypocrisy. The behavior of a big city superintendent who attended a satellite-downlinked telecommunications seminar with his top administrators reveals more than any of his rhetoric could about how power relationships work. On the one hand, he spoke of "shared leadership," "decentralized responsibility," and "empowerment" in his district. When everyone sat down to watch the presentation, however, he turned to one of his district principals. "Get me some coffee," he said, and the man hurried to serve. Later, having spilled some of the coffee, he whispered across to another of his lieutenants, "Get me some napkins." He, too, complied. The relationship of superintendent to administrators was clearly that of boss to worker, and nothing he could say about his larger vision of participation could erase the image of power that his actions conveyed. The same is true in the classroom, where relationships must be marked by mutual respect and where actions reflect the articulated and shared vision.

Shared vision is what gives people a sense of their own responsibilities and roles within organizations, from families to schools to corporations. A family planning a camping trip becomes a focused unit when its members prepare all winter: saving canned food, poring over new maps, and purchasing supplies. Each one envisions the vacation, and this vision provides the inspiration to make small sacrifices, contribute to the planning, and become involved in the success of the trip. For example, Emily, a child in a family planning such a vacation, saw herself as organizing her brother's suitcase and coordinating all the inflatables: beach balls, rafts, and a small boat. Armed with a small hand compressor, she was prepared to do her part to contribute to everyone's fun in the water.

Senge (1990) suggests that vision, "a force in people's hearts" rather than just an idea, shapes people's futures when they begin to see it as if it exists. In fact, it is through vision that the future is created. "Few if any forces in human affairs are as powerful as shared vision," he emphasizes (p. 206).

Students respond to shared vision as emphatically as do teachers. Told a number of years ago that there was no money to create a middle school literary magazine, and that they should instead submit their work to the high school magazine, *Aesthesia,* a small group of students at The Miami Valley School were determined not to let their vision die. They enlisted the voluntary help of a teacher to serve as advisor; they solicited student work, such as poems, drawings, and short stories; and they met after school to read them. They typed the selected works, sought printing funds from a variety of sources outside the school, met their deadlines, and ultimately produced a delightful product, wryly entitling it *AN-aesthesia.* Their vision became reality through their own leadership.

In fact, it is often student leadership that helps us to understand the power of shared vision. Students in a special program at Centerville (Ohio) High School envisioned a medieval banquet possibility and brought it to reality with the encouragement of their advisor. It involved researching authentic food, costume, and entertainment and persuading a local restaurant to let the group use a private banquet room (where they not only put straw on the floor but populated the room with chickens that wandered around in authentic medieval style throughout the meal). Each detail, from the decorations to the juggling act to a marauding horde that interrupted the meal, had been carefully studied and recreated, primarily with the enthusiasm, leadership, and resourcefulness of the students themselves.

The responsibility for guiding vision is critical to leadership's role. Leaders not only see the vision and have a clear idea of where the organization is going but also persist in the face of setbacks and failures. This persistence inspires others in the organization to persist rather than give up the vision, and thus is key to bringing it about. The leadership team in a school continues to reinforce the vision that every person can experience joy in learning. When there are setbacks, these leaders help to clear the way so that all members of the school can persist toward that vision. But "unless you know where you're going, and why, you cannot possibly get there" (Bennis 1989, 39–40). When poor Alice, lost in Wonderland, asked the Cheshire Cat which way she should go, he retorted, "It depends . . . on where you want to get to." When she said it really didn't matter, as long as she was going *somewhere,* his exasperating response was, "Then, it doesn't really matter *which* way you go," adding that she was sure to get there "if only you walk long enough." (*Lewis Carroll's Alice's adventures in wonderland* 1982, 79).

A passion for a vision

Leaders must not only share the vision for their systems, but they must also have passion for that vision and the will to create it. Without passion for what they are doing in the classroom, teachers wither and burn out. Whenever professionals lose sight of the vision—where are we going—the result is likely to be cynicism or a kind of going-through-the-motions approach to the task. (At a 1993 conference, author Alfie Kohn, describing a teacher who is intrinsically motivated and highly enthusiastic about her job, asks rhetorically, "Is *this* the teacher whose car will bear the bumper sticker message, 'Work sucks, but I need the bucks'?")

The trick is to stay in touch with the vision, and this means staying in touch with customers. At The Miami Valley School, the headmaster spends a certain amount of time at community cultivation luncheons, where he meets leaders of the community—not school parents—to share his vision of the school and to articulate its role within the whole community. This role is essential to the success of the school's vision. It provides immediate feedback from disinterested members of the community and offers an opportunity to communicate the school's vision to these customers.

For the vision to be vital, the same kind of communication must go on with internal customers as well. If teachers and principals do not share the school's vision, the community visits will represent only isolated marketing forays rather than reflecting the fabric of the school. In many school systems, it is clear that understanding the school's vision is distinctly different for parents, taxpayers, teachers, and students. A leader's role is to integrate the sense of vision to assure that the system is moving in the same direction for all of its customers.

One way in which the vision itself, as well as passion for that vision, can be sustained lies in the understanding that everyone is part of a larger system. The classroom teacher feels alliances and partnerships with other teachers, with the administrative function of the school, with the community in which the school operates, with the nation, the world, and the universe. The idealism of young teachers is often rooted in this sense of the global impact of their vocation. Teacher-in-space Krista McAuliffe's assertion, "I touch the future. I teach," resounded in every educator's heart.

In an educational system, the role of leadership is to sustain the vision of connectedness, so that students, teachers, administrators, parents, and taxpayers—all those who receive the benefit of the system—understand their roles with respect to the larger systems of learning in which they operate. Poet Walt Whitman (1856) asserted his connectedness with past and present, rich and poor, and men and women in "Crossing Brooklyn Ferry." In the same ways, schools must see themselves as part of an ongoing process of learning and of continuous improvement, with connections to customers both present and future and to the culture of which they are a part.

This is a daunting responsibility, especially in the face of failed tax levies, state minimum requirements, absence policies, and standardized tests. Leaders can create strategic alliances and partnerships that will help them to focus on the large implications of what they do; this, too, is their responsibility to their systems. Leaders "see the world globally, and they know it is no longer possible to hide" (Bennis 1989, 201). While this global cooperation is the loftiest alliance, leaders can foster cooperation within their systems in order to sustain vision. In fact, cooperation may be the only way in which vision can be sustained. Instead of bashing taxpayers, school leaders might approach them with vision.

A dynamic web

The dynamic web of relationships that reflects the new world view is suggested in modern physics. The old mechanistic physics of Newton has been replaced by an understanding of the world in terms articulated by Einstein and others in quantum physics. This approach not only presents a new understanding of matter, but also gives a physical basis for a more holistic and less fragmented way of seeing ourselves in the world (Zohar 1990). The world view posited by quantum physics represents a powerful metaphor for the ways in which educational systems can be reengineered to respond to the complex world of which they are a part. Optimism generated by a world view of interdependence and dynamic growth is reflected in the vision of students working together in common purpose, cooperating for mutual learning, and challenging one another to higher creativity. The smallest group of students working together to design and build a set for a play mirrors the world as we want our children to know it.

People clearly need what Laszlo (1974, 9) calls a "sense of purpose beyond one's own narrow interests," and they will respond to purposeful challenges because the purpose is what gives meaning to work. When a custodian at NASA's Houston headquarters was asked what his job was, he replied, "To put a man on the moon." He was expressing the vision of the organization in terms of his own participation in that vision. This was a personal vision as well (Barth 1988). It is the responsibility of an organization's leadership to communicate the vision, keep a focus on it, and foster movement toward its fulfillment. It is the responsibility of everyone in the organization to understand the vision and translate it into a sense of purpose for every job. Without a sense of purpose and a clear vision related to the organization, those who are part of that organization will identify only with their own individual goals rather than see themselves as important to the big picture.

In the classroom, when students without systems knowledge or an understanding of purpose are asked how to improve the system within which they find themselves, they are likely to respond with suggestions like "shorter classes," "gum in classes," "longer lunches," "more vacation," or "more free time." When students share the same vision, however, and a sense of purpose is part of their experience, they are more likely to respond, as they did in one school, with "more history classes," "longer class periods," "expanded hours for the computer room," "advanced physics," and "community service opportunities." These students have taken ownership of the system and responsibility for their own learning. They no longer need the teacher or principal to say, "You need more history," "Class periods should be extended," or "All students will spend more time learning computer technology."

Style and structure

Social psychologist Kurt Lewin's (1989) early experiments in social situations and leadership styles suggested three types of leadership. Students in groups led with an autocratic style worked hardest (but only when they were watched), and had the highest levels of aggressive and hostile behavior. A laissez-faire kind of leadership, with total freedom and no guidance, resulted in few accomplishments by the group, and poorest quality of work among the three types. A democratically led group, on the other hand, produced a group with the highest levels of motivation and originality, and also, interestingly enough, the greatest sense of playfulness and fun in its work.

In any system, quality learning does not mean abandoning leadership or turning everything over to the system's participants without guidance. It means helping all members to define the system, understand their roles in it, and see ways in which processes can be improved. Participation in articulating the purpose of the organization is important to this end. Without this understanding, efforts aimed at empowering them—literally, sharing the power to suddenly run the organization—are doomed to failure, even if everyone were to have the specific skills required to manage day-to-day operations. It is vision, and the understanding of purpose, that give a system's members confidence to contribute to improvement. "Without vision, the people perish," Proverbs 28 assures us.

Structure in an organization that is committed to enhancing the learning of all of its members is dynamic, not rigid. Nineteenth-century American writers identified the structures of human experience with the structures of nature. A plant, for example, sprouts new shoots in a way that is not at all like those of other plants; no two are the same and yet each has its own, organic pattern. That pattern is not always discernible, but has its own structure. "Nature's dice are always loaded . . . in her heaps and rubbish are concealed sure and useful results" (Emerson, 1842).

As in plants that grow in apparently random ways, what may appear to be lack of structure in organizations is often, in fact, a dynamic sense of changing roles and relationships in order to carry out the purpose of that organization. When people are locked into rigid titles and their names appear on traditional organizational charts in little boxes that report to other, higher-up little boxes, their sense of their own roles as dynamic and expanding is seriously inhibited. On the other hand, students who see the structure of the classroom as one that supports open exchange of ideas and understands failure as one way of learning, will feel that they are members of an expanding, learning organization rather than a closed, punitive one.

Organizations that depend on rigid, hierarchical structures and bureaucratic relationships among people inhibit their members' ability to contribute to the organization's goals. Structure, as Peter Senge (1990) points out, produces behavior. He defines structure not as that shown on an organizational chart. Instead, "systemic structure is concerned with the key relationships that influence behavior over time."

Margaret Wheatley (1992) suggests that although our scientific view of the universe has shifted from that of Newtonian physics to twentieth-century understandings of quantum physics, our organizations remain fixed in the Newtonian paradigm. The notion of organizations, and the universe itself, as machinelike and rigid is a vestige of Newtonian thinking. Instead, these may be seen as combinations of key patterns and principles that "express the system's overall identity"—or what we have called purpose.

Today's organizations, after restructuring, reengineering, downsizing, and other processes described in characteristic euphemism, have implicitly recognized the changing role of leadership. *Transformational leadership, servant leadership,* and *distributed leadership,* are not simply the flavors of the month, but terms that challenge the definition of leadership that is required for organizations in a changed world. What *FORTUNE* (Huey 1994) calls "post-heroic leadership" reflects the changing structure of organizations to less hierarchical, more horizontal, less-is-more systems. "It's about managing across, not up and down," asserts *Business Week* (Byrne 1993). A decade ago, soon after publication of *A Nation at Risk* and its indictment of the American educational system, Chester Finn Jr. (1984) articulated the tension between school-level autonomy and systemwide uniformity, and described appropriate school leadership as largely site-based and school-level, with more budgetary and hiring prerogatives granted to individual schools and their teachers. Of course if local control is to come about, those who lead the schools from boards of education must have access to innovative thinkers in the profession. The learning organization must include all of its members, so that leaders are not basing their approaches on obsolete paradigms (Theobald 1982).

Vision as a motivator

When a little girl became trapped in a well in Texas a few years ago, her plight commanded national attention. Rescue attempts focused on a variety of ways to enter the shaft and release the child without injury. It was determined that a special piece of equipment used in mining was needed, and the urgency meant that it would have to be shipped immediately from a location in another state. In order to make such a delivery happen, the overnight air delivery organization ordinarily required approval from a supervisor. That requirement notwithstanding, a dispatcher bypassed the approval process and got the equipment delivered within hours.

"How did you do that without risking your job?" the dispatcher was asked.

"I know my company has confidence in my ability to make judgments in an emergency situation and that they will stand behind me," was the reply.

The leadership in that organization is clear; the source of the employee's empowerment did not lie in company policy, but in an atmosphere of confidence and trust that was part of the organization's culture.

That atmosphere was created because all employees shared a common vision of the company's purpose.

Shared leadership and teamwork

Understanding teamwork and encouraging contributions from all members of the organization represent a kind of shared leadership. That is, leadership qualities are developed at all levels of an organization—not just at the top. Administrators of systems recognize leadership within the framework of teams. Sometimes a distinction is made between working *in* the system and working *on* it. In any system, managers of that system work *on* it to bring about improvement for those who work *in* it. That is, these managers—school administrators, for example—must clear the obstacles to improvement when they lie within their control to do so. Letting go is frequently the most difficult lesson leaders can learn.

An American business leader who visited Japan with President George Bush early in 1992 commented with some condescension about the emphasis on teamwork in manufacturing in that culture. His comments reflected American values for individualism, independence, and resourcefulness. The tone of his comments implied a higher value in "doing it yourself" than in having to depend on others. Our how-many-does-it-take-to-change-a-lightbulb jokes may reflect our culture's vague mistrust of team activity; we believe that competent people are those who somehow complete tasks alone.

It is clear that leadership as an its-lonely-at-the-top endeavor is quite different from that of one in which the leaders' role is to support others as they work to improve the organization of which they are a part. This is true for teachers as well as school administrators. A Bridgeport, Connecticut, English teacher found herself one fall in the 1960s in a classroom facing 42 eighth graders with varying levels of interest in learning anything at all about English. Her primary function was to instruct these young people so that they would all be able to do the same work, albeit at varying levels of skill. To keep order, she used her voice—a somewhat ineffective instrument in a room that included 18-year-olds who couldn't yet read. Her colleague across the hall used more direct approaches, often physical, to achieve this end. Both found that they might be able to keep their classes reasonably quiet, but with 42 students in a room, it was indeed impossible to really teach anything having to do with iambic pentameter, indefinite pronouns, or the basics of spelling. As class size increases, the autocratic leaders' effectiveness is proportionately diminished.

If, on the other hand, a classroom were organized in such a way that students supported and facilitated each other's learning, the number of students would be a far less significant factor. In Leander, Texas, for example, more than 150 fifth graders worked in the same large room to accomplish learning tasks that they had selected. Were they quiet? Hardly. But as self-managed groups, the students were learning to focus on their work in meaningful ways, to listen to each other's ideas, and to produce an outcome upon which they agreed. Without imposed structures and schedules, students took breaks as they needed to (without anyone's permission), but their work continued without interruption. In addition to gaining competence with concepts and skills related to the social science project on which they were working, the fifth graders were learning fundamental skills of working together, concentrating without becoming distracted by other groups' activities, and utilizing contributions from everyone in the group. Individual student learning was enhanced by group processes that brought out the best in everyone. They were not competing for individual goals, but cooperating to enhance the learning of everyone.

The rugged individual: An American myth

The value that our culture places on the independent efforts of the individual rather than on group achievement is sometimes considered a product of our frontier beginnings, forged by the isolated living and dangerous environments in which pioneers found themselves. In the mode of survival of the individual that the pioneer's environment at times demanded, there was no leisure for consideration of others' possible contributions to the decision-making process, or for building group problem-solving skills. Instead, exigency demanded that individual leaders take charge, make decisions quickly and effectively, and expect others to follow.

James Fenimore Cooper's ([1823–1841] 1895–1900) mythic Natty Bumppo character created a definition of leadership for generations of Americans. A rugged outdoorsman, Bumppo's physical prowess and his understanding of his natural environment contributed not only to his own survival in nature but also to his ability to help (indeed, to rescue) others, who, without these gifts, became dependent on his leadership for their own survival. In his series of Leatherstocking stories, Cooper created a kind of frontier knight, who was able to survive the rigors of nature by dint of his superior strength and skill. This nation's romance with the American frontier has rendered the rugged Cooper character a model of what it means to solve problems.

In crisis situations, both on the frontier and in the heat of battle, it has indeed been these skills of quick thinking and decisive action that have defined leaders. Those who could not give orders were simply followers. The same mode can be seen in other crisis situations as well. When a military battalion is attacked by enemy fire, for example, orders must be centralized, quick, and effective, and others must be prepared to follow those orders. There is a kind of cause-effect relationship between the individual and the outcome or solution of the problem at hand.

Of course, the emphasis on frontier individualism is based to a great extent on myth rather than reality. For most settlers in the West, for example, immediate crisis was the exception rather than the rule. For the most part, getting things done involved not just the resourcefulness of the individual, but teamwork among members of a community. This is how towns were settled, barns were built, livestock was branded, and crops were harvested. One family helped another, not just in crises of health or fortune, but in the management of economic demands as well. Like nests of ants or hives of bees, the model of natural cooperation demonstrates the potential accomplishments of those working together. Whether they realized what was happening or not, it is clear that by cooperating, settlers were able to accomplish far more as groups than they could have hoped to bring about as individuals. Nonetheless, abetted by such views as that of the eighteenth-century French aristocrat St. Jean de Crevecoeur as well as Rousseau's idealization of natural man, the myth of the rugged individual, surviving by dint of his or her own resourcefulness and wit alone, isolated from society, has persisted and made its stamp on the American character. Crevecoeur, in fact, praised the resourcefulness of American farmers who lived by their own wits and conquered adverse fortune seemingly alone.

Whether the frontier demanded it or not, certainly the effectiveness of the model of individualistic leadership through crisis, with its concomitant competitive spirit, gives way when it comes to survival in an increasingly interdependent world. Complexity alone demands that individuals share leadership in a variety of ways and depend on the resources that are available rather than relying only on themselves to solve problems. Whether an industrial-era set of attitudes is appropriate to the new set of conditions that organizations face today is a question that must be asked (Theobald 1982).

Leadership and control

In a school district in Alaska, a new principal, wanting to demonstrate her leadership skills, devised an elaborate plan for transporting itinerant teachers from village to village. The teachers, who had lived and worked in the area for several years, listened to her presentation. Then without hesitation they told her that although her plan looked good on paper, the climatic conditions of Alaska's great land would never allow the plan to succeed. Abruptly, she dismissed their contributions as a threat to her authority and the plan went forward.

Four months later, after winter had set in, the group was starting over, devising an entirely new plan based on input from the local teachers. The principal's style of management, in which leaders are expected to do rather than lead, had cost the district thousands of dollars and the loss of four months' time. The principal, however, felt the need to control the process and saw leadership in these terms.

Human resources consultant Stephen Covey (1989) suggests that effective leaders recognize the pattern of human development—the movement from dependence to independence to interdependence—as one of growth, not of increasing weakness. Yet, in the traditional American emphasis on competition, it is independence that is fostered, rather than awareness of the interactive dependencies that make systems work. Managers in a total quality school work to assure interdependence and shared vision, and to improve the system that serves that shared vision. Teachers, as managers of classrooms, can foster this interdependence and facilitate group learning, which enhances individual learning as well.

A language teacher gave a traditional vocabulary test to her students. She graded the test, recorded the grades, and gave the tests back to the students. A week later, without warning, she administered the same test to the students, assuring them that these grades would not count, but represented a way to check the quality of their learning. Scores were substantially lower, confirming her suspicion that the class had learned the words only for the test. For the next vocabulary mastery test, students were expecting the same kind of exam the teacher had given before. This time, however, after she passed out the tests, she told the students they could work in groups of three or four to answer the test questions; scores would count for all members of each group. Elated, the students eagerly quizzed each other and recorded the best answers to each question. Their scores were predictably higher than they had been on previous tests—even for those who had not prepared at all for the test.

A week later, again unannounced, the teacher gave the same test to the class. This time, students worked individually, and their tests were then graded. The test scores on these tests reflected higher retention levels than those of the tests given earlier without the benefit of the teamwork exercise. Although the outcomes were inconclusive—based on only one set of students and two different tests—the results led the teacher to believe that her students learned better in group settings than as individuals. As a leader in the classroom, she shared her observations with her students, seeking their reactions to her experiment. A unpredicted result of the discussion was the enhanced interest the students began to take in their own learning. Asking, how can we learn vocabulary best, the students proposed and carried out a variety of testing situations, including traditional exams, oral exchanges, and creative demonstrations of mastery. Unlike the Alaska principal in the earlier example, the language teacher did not see leadership in terms of control of the process, but instead as an opportunity to develop students' own sense of leadership and responsibility.

The leadership that this teacher demonstrated reflected her confidence in her students' willingness to improve their mastery of their learning and their ability to change the classroom system to demonstrate this mastery. She effectively enlarged what Covey refers to as people's "circle of influence" (see Figure 8.1). This circle contains the things peo-

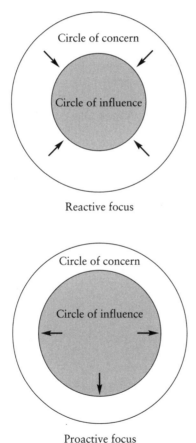

Figure 8.1: Covey's circles.

ple can do something about or have control over. The language teacher was diminishing the students' circle of concern, which Covey says includes those matters over which people have no control or influence. Covey distinguishes reactive from proactive leadership by suggesting that those who focus only on the circle of concern approach circumstances over which they have no control by blaming, criticizing others, and becoming victims. The proactive focus concentrates on those things that can be changed, and is energetic, positive, and magnifying. It actually enlarges the circle of influence.

Leadership and failure

When things go wrong, the individualistic and competitive society in which we live wants to find fault—preferably with a person who has caused a failure. This behavior occurs in the circle of concern area, where people focus on others' weaknesses and other problems over which they have no control, but which create difficulty in their own lives.

Classroom teachers cannot directly understand or address the problems that lie in the school's purchasing department, for example, but this aspect of the school's operation affects what happens in those teachers' classrooms. If book orders are not issued by the business office in time, students will be without texts on the first day of school. This is not the teachers' fault, and yet it may very directly affect the opportunities for learning in the classroom. One kind of leadership encourages teachers to complain bitterly about the business office, knowing that they can do nothing about it. Another kind of leadership encourages everyone in the system to consider themselves members of the same team, and to work together on common problems. The teachers' insight about book-order problems may not take into account some aspects of those problems, but it nonetheless represents a valid contribution toward improving the book-order system.

Recognizing failures as opportunities for growth is one of the characteristics that distinguishes real leadership from mere supervision. Enlightened leaders look for opportunities to support, to get out of the way, and to identify the resources necessary for people to do their jobs well. Leaders work with employees to improve processes, rather than criticizing workers for failures in the system, recognizing that the people who know the job best are the ones who actually do it. The strategy works not only for districtwide school leaders but also for classroom leadership provided by teachers.

Leadership represents a kind of enlightened position in an organization or group. Leaders are those who can see, who can use shared experience to bear on problem-solving and planning activities in the group. Deming (1986) distinguishes between this role and that of supervisors, or those whose role is not to see, but to control. Among other contrasts that he suggests are the supervisors' propensities to judge, to "oversee," to base actions on results, while leaders learn from available data, support others as colleagues in doing their jobs, diminish fear by focusing on improvement of the system rather than blaming individuals, and actively coach and counsel those in the system.

It is important to emphasize that when leaders adopt a style of collaboration and support, they are not giving up responsibilities that are fundamental to the role of administrative leader. While the new approach seems distinctly warm and fuzzy, it, in fact, puts a greater burden on the administrators with respect to those who do not contribute to the vision of the organization. Look at an example.

In a power-leadership structure, for employees who are seen as weak performers or whose contributions are questionable (but apparently not bad enough to justify dismissal), the administrators might vent frustration in the annual performance review, citing all the failings they have observed during the past year. Some of the most caustic language around is that half-damning annual indictment from frustrated principals who don't know how to "make" employees improve. Concomitant to that review might be a half-hearted salary increase (if that is within the leader's control)—say, 3 percent if the average were 7 percent, or the withholding of merit pay. It might take the form of assigning difficult teaching schedules, or undesirable extra-curricular assignments. ("But I've been on early-morning bus duty for 17 years!") It might even be expressed in general exhortation or veiled threat to the entire group, "Faculty attendance at arts assemblies must improve, or something will have to be done about it." The leaders' hope is that the employees will become frustrated with the pay or conditions and leave the organization. Usually what happens when this approach is adopted is that the employees stay, but become increasingly cynical and bitter, sapping energy from the organization by continuing to work there. The circle of concern becomes larger, and the circle of influence becomes smaller.

On the other hand, genuine leadership in a quality organization will be reflected in ongoing modelling of valued behaviors and coaching toward improvement in all areas. When someone is part of a team and fails to contribute, the team itself will become part of the coaching process, but the supervisors will support that process. They will immediately notice positive and negative accomplishments and give feedback about them right away, rather than saving them for the gunny sack of the annual performance review. ("I noticed that you were not at the arts assembly today, Mr. Strom. You missed the last one as well. How can I help you to get to the assemblies?" or "I'm happy that you have an interest in the theory of multiple intelligences. Perhaps you'll want to attend a conference this summer.") When behavior does not change in spite of repeated efforts to coach and train, the leaders' responsibility is ultimately to do whatever it takes to remove those employees from the organization or to diminish their role in it.

In the same way that principals or superintendents reinforce the efforts of teachers and make it possible for them to do their jobs and grow as members of a learning organization, teachers support the improvement of students in the classroom, providing leadership and facilitation to the learning process. These students will be at different stages in their learning, and teachers must help them identify what they know and lead their efforts to improve. To do this, the teachers, like the principals or superintendents, have a knowledge of how systems work, an understanding of variation within systems, a clear sense of the theory upon which learning is based, and an appreciation for the psychology of human behavior—particularly that of the young people in the classroom and of the ways in which they learn.

Dynamic leadership

Comparing leadership styles of successful military, religious, political, and corporate leaders demonstrates that the concept of leadership is a dynamic one. Leadership styles reflect the purpose of the organization as well as the historical times in which they are exercised. Medieval ecclesiastical authority prevailed over a populace characterized by limited education and economic resources, in an age where communication was restricted by geography and lack of common language. The authoritarian hierarchy was perhaps the most appropriate model of leadership for the time. Likewise, governmental authority that evolves in times of crisis has its particular hallmark. The D-day invasion could never have taken place without centralized, unquestioned authority. Perhaps it is not too much to expect that leadership in the twenty-first century can reflect the needs of the times. Its population will be healthier and better educated than those of other times and places, and its problems will be more complex than ever. A new and perhaps more complex leadership style is indeed called for in our time.

Historically, our schools have, for the most part, provided a quality education for the society in which they have existed, and their leadership provided the style that reflected this society's requirements. Most graduates could expect to find themselves in hierarchical organizations (similar to classroom environments), where they would be rewarded for doing what they were told to do without understanding or contributing to the company vision. Most dropouts could find jobs that did not require more than minimal skill levels. A society with greater numbers of jobs that do not require technological expertise or higher educational levels can afford dropouts from its schools more comfortably than nations with fewer manufacturing facilities, higher levels of entry-level expertise, and more emphasis on higher-order thinking skills.

Today, organizations operate with increasing need for creative thinking skills; the ability to get along with and work productively with others in team situations; enhanced communication skills; and expanded technological know-how. Unlike the traditional factory job where workers are trained to do repetitive tasks, today's companies depend on schools to produce graduates with the ability to adapt to changing environments and demands, and to analyze and assess information. Narrowly defined vocational training skills are no longer sufficient. Leadership must change to meet these changing demands. Leadership in the classroom can support students' need to deal with the complex rather than focusing on simple solutions.

Creating an atmosphere for leadership

Society at large needs citizens with these skills as well, in order to have a positive impact on social and political institutions and to plan for future generations. Yet even our best school districts continue to produce students trained for the needs of the past rather than for the future. Regardless of what our vision may be, or how hard we work to bring it about, we can never reach it by using the same approaches we are already using. We can declare that we will reduce dropout rates in this nation by 20 percent before the turn of the century; but just trying harder with the same methods we've already tried will never make this happen. Certainly, simply saying we will accomplish something will not bring it about.

Leaders in schools must develop knowledge for themselves and for others in the organization; leaders must sustain passion for the vision and schools must become learning organizations in every way. This implies trust and elimination of fear, as Deming emphasizes in his 14 points for managers. These points provide a kind of road map to managers who want to adopt the new philosophy of leadership that has evolved from the ideas of Deming and other management theorists. *Evolved* is the key description. Deming himself revised his list several times; the list itself did not exist when he first began studying organizations, but grew out of his awareness of statistical methods and his observation of management leadership failures.

These points, adapted from Deming to reflect the language of schools, are as follows:

1. Create constancy of purpose toward improvement of students and service. Aim to create the best-quality students capable of improving all forms of processes and entering meaningful positions in society.
2. Adopt the new philosophy. Educational management must awaken to the challenge, must learn its responsibilities, and must take on leadership for change.
3. Work to abolish grading and the harmful effects of rating people. Cease dependence on testing to achieve quality. Eliminate the need for inspections on a mass basis (standardized achievement tests, minimum graduation exams, and so on) by providing learning experiences that create quality performance.
4. Work with the educational institutions from which students come. Minimize total cost of education by improving the relationship with student sources and helping to improve the quality of students coming into the system. A single source of students coming into a system, such as junior-high students moving into a high school, is an opportunity to build long-term relationships of loyalty and trust for the benefit of students.
5. Improve, constantly and forever, the system of student learning and service, to improve quality and productivity.
6. Institute education and training on the job for students, teachers, classified staff, and administrators.
7. Adopt and institute leadership. The aim of supervision should be to help people use machines, gadgets, and materials to do a better job. Technology frees leaders to lead.
8. Drive out fear so that everyone may work effectively for the school system. Create an environment that encourages people to speak freely.
9. Break down barriers between departments. People in teaching, special education, accounting, food service, administration, curriculum development and research, and so on must work as a team. Develop strategies for increasing the cooperation among groups and individual people.
10. Eliminate slogans, exhortations, and targets for teachers and students, asking for perfect performance and new levels of productivity. Exhortations create adversarial relationships. The bulk of the causes of low quality and low productivity belong to the system and thus lie beyond the control of teachers and students.

11. Eliminate work standards (quotas) on teachers and students (for example, "raise test scores by 10 percent," or "lower drop-out rates by 15 percent"). Substitute leadership.

12. Remove barriers that rob students, teachers, and management (principals, superintendents, and central office support staff) of their right to pride and joy of workmanship. This means, *inter alia,* abolition of the annual or merit rating and of management by objective. The responsibility of all educational managers must be changed from quantity to quality.

13. Institute a vigorous program of education and self-improvement for everyone.

14. Put everybody in the school community to work to accomplish the transformation.

From detection to prevention

With an understanding of improvement theory developed, appreciation for systems advanced, variation in processes accounted for, and the people issues based on psychology in place, management's job is no longer to direct or police. The role has changed from one of detection (of errors, goof-ups, and inconsistencies) to one of prevention and support. What management gains is a new ability to predict and to understand when a system is stable, and when it is unstable and in need of attention.

Of course, teachers as well as administrators are managers. In the classroom, teachers gain an understanding of variation in student performance, and can direct their efforts to improving the performance of the entire system rather than ranking students within the limits of common causes for variation. Natural variation occurs in any process. We don't expect popcorn kernels to pop all at once, or consider those that pop first to be superior in some way. This variation seems to be quite acceptable. But as we have seen, classroom performance has its own variation. Students may all reach the same level eventually, but unlike the kernels of popcorn, young people are evaluated on the basis of their teachers' judgment of where they are at a given point in the popping process.

Leadership is not the realm of only those in administrative offices, but is shared in the deepest sense. This means far more than delegating or discussing important decisions with others. It means believing first, then translating belief into reality. "If you have built castles in the air, your work need not be lost; that is where they should be. Now put the foundations under them" (Thoreau 1854). When the organization's vision is shared and communicated, what ensues is a new community of leaders that includes not just the superintendent, but teachers and students as well.

Leadership and joy in work

In considering the input of those within the system, it must be remembered that most people—students, teachers, principals, and superintendents—want to do a good job. No one gets up in the morning and goes to work determined to do a bad job. The system must foster the need for people to find satisfaction in their work so that they will continue to want to be successful at whatever they do. Even the worst employees did not begin their careers trying to prove how terrible they could be. Everyone wants to contribute and to feel productive and useful. The more that the positive efforts of people can be recognized, the more we will see them concentrating on improving.

The old boss management (Glasser 1990) operated on the basic principle that people will try to get away with murder if they can. Therefore, they have to be watched and inspected to assure they are doing what they are supposed to. Control is the leadership style consistent with this principle. The quality philosophy assumes that all people want to be involved and to do their jobs well. In the classroom, a continuum of relationships describes the move from "do to" leadership to a "do with" style (see Figure 8.2).

In the educational systems of our nation, top-down management has been the hallmark since the early days of universal public education—or at least since the days of consolidated school districts whose numbers seemed to require this style of management. (In earlier days, after all, the one-room schoolhouse operated on the principle of site-based management and a nearly flat organizational structure.) Boards of education, those representatives of the community elected not because of their expertise but by virtue of their interest, are looked to not only for their vision of community education but also for their power. Board members are approached to solve a variety of internal problems and address matters that they are ill-equipped to understand. It is because of the pyramid organization of the schools that a board of education's role is so frequently misunderstood. The assumption seems to be that because board members are at the top, they must know enough to run their organizations. Built into such an organizational shape is the ingredient of fear. School administrators are afraid of the ramifications of their decisions and often cannot count on support from above.

With power residing at the top (in schools, with the board of education), the clear message is one of diminished leadership at all levels. John Carver, leadership consultant to not-for-profit boards of directors,

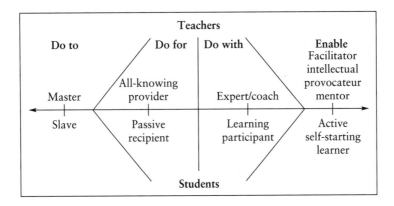

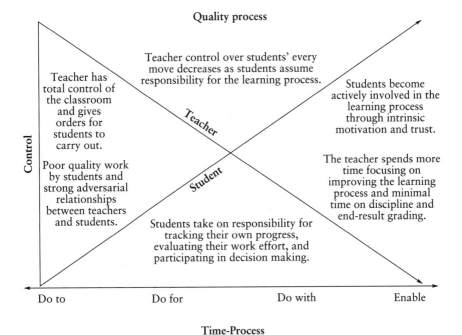

Figure 8.2: Student-teacher relationship spectrum.

quips that such boards are often composed of highly successful, highly effective people who are rendered incompetent when they are put in a room together to make decisions about an organization in which they do not work.

Traditional organizational charts do not account for the complexity of leadership nor for the enlightened understanding of individuals at all levels of an organization. The role of teachers is unique in a school system, at once delivering the school's services and supporting its vision. Teachers understand the school's customers best, by being at the heart of a system of service delivery and regularly accepting students from internal suppliers; by shaping a classroom to serve the needs of those customers; and by then becoming suppliers for other customers in the students' ensuing years of school. Teachers themselves—and students—in an atmosphere of trust and empowerment, can shape the vision for schools. This atmosphere of trust is not fostered in a top-down hierarchical power base, however, where fear and barriers to change are identified with the ultimate power that resides at the top. Rather than a pyramid construction, it has been suggested that an upside-down pyramid best describes a quality organization. Thus, the administrators are at the bottom in order to support the efforts of those above them.

Power-leadership destroys joy

A consultant to industry tells a story about his summer-employment days at a large American automobile assembly plant at New Jersey during his college years. A bright 18-year-old eager to do well and to please, he noticed a number of things about his job of installing a particular screw that secured a windshield-wiper button. The tool that he was issued to tighten the screw was not exactly the right dimension, and as a result every fourth or fifth screw was stripped and sheared off. He also saw that if he could stand in a slightly different place when the car bodies moved down the assembly line he could improve his productivity and decrease the amount of walking back and forth encountered on the job.

Though he was confident in most ways, the young man approached his supervisor only with great diffidence. He had seen the older man fire people on the spot (he himself had already been yelled at for reading a book during a lull on the assembly line), and the older man's blustery, crude language was a source of some intimidation to the workers under him. Nonetheless, believing that he could indeed produce better work with only a few minor changes, he one day summoned the courage to approach his boss with his suggestions. During a break, he caught the supervisor in a moment of apparent pause, and decided to mention the tool problem to him.

The supervisor looked at the young man, first in disbelief, then in anger. "When we need something from you, I'll be the one to tell you about it!" he yelled, adding, with a flavoring of expletives, "Now get back to your station."

The college student was a quick learner. He indeed never mentioned another of his ideas to his boss. The tool continued to shear screw shafts at the rate of about 20 percent. The young man gave up caring. (Later,

as a consultant, the man pointed out the irony in his years-afterward return to the assembly site, finding it had been torn down and replaced by
a new, modern Japanese auto-assembly plant. The only one of the original buildings still standing was a motor pool garage, where a tattered
poster still hung, its invisible voice-from-above admonishing long-gone
workers, "To all foremen: We are not interested in *why* it can't be done.
The Management.") When the consultant tells the story now to leaders
of industry, most nod, ruefully understanding what was wrong with the
situation. Yet schools reenact this story on a daily basis in their management styles. Fear is indeed a powerful motivator, but one is never sure
exactly what it motivates people to do.

With top-down leadership and implicit structures of fear, school systems have the same effect on teachers as the overbearing supervisor had
on the college student. Professional burnout, bitterness, quarrels over
contracts, and limitations on what teachers can be required to do—these
characterize the modern school system where professionals have lost
their joy in work, as surely as the bright, eager five-year-olds will often
lose their sense of joy in creativity and learning long before graduation
from the public education system.

On the other hand, when members of an organization share a vision
and a common sense of purpose, and see themselves as part of a system,
working within it to improve the entire system to service the needs of
society, they no longer use the pronoun *they*. Instead, these organizational members have a clear sense of *we*, where teachers, students, community members, administrators, and staff work together to bring
about improvement. The customer focus—understanding the needs of
the society that receives our graduates—provides the "so what?" of the
methods we pursue to improve. If all schools are providing students for
this customer, they must cooperate to identify the ultimate requirements
of society now and in the future. This understanding is not only fundamental to producing quality students for the market that awaits them in
the universities, workplaces, and communities, but it also helps to establish the customer-supplier partnership between society and its
schools. It is only with such understanding that genuine and long-term
changes can be made that will bring about the improvement of schools
for the students of this generation and the next.

Leadership for quality

Imparting the vision clearly to all members of an organization is what
leadership is all about. Encouraging them to have pride in their own
contributions to the vision is equally important. And working with
them to make the vision of the organization their own will assure beau-

tiful music. A principal can support a fifth-grade teacher's fledgling efforts with cooperative learning, criticize an athletic director's failure to schedule enough home games, or encourage a music teacher with plans for a fine arts festival, all in the context of the school's vision. The principal could do it without reference to the vision as well, but each interaction provides an opportunity to reinforce that vision and to solidify the teachers' sense of contribution to the school's purpose and vision.

Vision, like the creation of a fine performance, involves translating what is known to be the purpose of an organization into an understanding of one's contribution to that purpose. By having vision we create our own future. And as futurist Joel Barker (1989) emphasizes, if we fail to create our own futures, someone else will.

In addition to understanding and communicating a sense of purpose to members of the organization, it is essential that the new leadership understand the improvement process that will produce appropriate responses to that purpose—the plan-do-study-act cycle described in chapter 5. This is true in any organization, since quality improvement demands theory, process, and tools regardless of whether we are talking about the classroom, the food line, or a construction project.

A particular vision is unique to an organization. One school may envision itself as providing opportunities for active learning for all of its members; but when another school attempts to spark vision by imitating this idea, it will undoubtedly fall flat. In a final look at learning and quality, chapter 9 will examine the idea of vision as it relates to the entire educational experience.

Notes

Barker, Joel. 1989. *Discovering the future: The business of paradigms.* Produced and directed by R. J. Christensen, B. W. Neal, and J. R. Christensen. 40 min. Burnsville, Minn.: Infinity Limited and Charthouse Learning. Videotape.

Barth, Roland S. 1988. Principals, teachers, and school leadership. *Phi Delta Kappan* (May): 639–642.

Bennis, Warren. 1989. *On becoming a leader.* Reading, Mass.: Addison-Wesley.

Byrne, John. 1993. The horizontal corporation. *Business Week,* 20 December, 76–81.

Cooper, James Fenimore. [1823–1841] 1895–1900. *The works of James Fenimore Cooper.* New York: Putnam.

Covey, Stephen R. 1989. *The seven habits of highly effective people: Powerful lessons in personal change.* New York: Fireside Books.

Deming, W. Edwards. 1986. *Out of the crisis*. Cambridge, Mass.: MIT Center for Advanced Engineering Study. Excerpts reprinted from *Out of the Crisis* by permission of MIT and W. Edwards Deming. Copyright 1986 by W. Edwards Deming.

Emerson, Ralph Waldo. [1842] 1950. Nature. In *Selected writings of Ralph Waldo Emerson,* edited by Brooks Atkinson. New York: Modern Library Editions.

Finn, Chester, E., Jr. 1984. Toward strategic independence: Nine commandments for enhancing school effectiveness. *Phi Delta Kappan 65*, no. 8:518–524.

Glasser, William. 1990. *The quality school: Managing students without coercion.* New York: Harper & Row.

Huey, John. 1994. The new post-heroic leadership. *FORTUNE,* 21 February, 42–50.

Laszlo, Ervin. 1974. *A strategy for the future: The systems approach to world order.* New York: George Brazillier.

Lewin, Kurt. 1989. *The power of the situation.* The Developments in Psychology series. Produced and directed by WGBH/Boston. Produced by Tug Yourgrad. Directed by Kim Story. 30 min. Videotape.

Lewis Carroll's Alice's Adventures in Wonderland. The Pennyroyal Edition. 1982. Designed and illustrated by Barry Moser. Berkeley, Calif.: University of California Press.

Sarason, S. B. 1990. *The predictable failure of educational reform.* San Francisco: Jossey-Bass.

Senge, Peter. 1990. *The fifth discipline: The art and practice of the learning organization.* New York: Doubleday.

Theobald, R. 1982. *Avoiding 1984: Moving toward interdependence.* Chicago: Swallow Press.

Thoreau, Henry David. [1854] 1960. *Walden, or life in the woods.* New York: New American Library.

Wheatley, Margaret J. 1992. *Leadership and the new science: Learning about organizations from an orderly universe.* San Francisco: Barrett-Koehler Publishers.

Whitman, Walt. [1856] 1950. Crossing Brooklyn ferry. In *Leaves of grass and selected prose.* New York: Modern Library Edition.

Zohar, D. 1990. *The quantum self: Human nature and consciousness defined by the new physics.* New York: William Morrow & Company.

Chapter 9

A Vision for Schools

If your plan is for one year, plant rice; if your plan is for ten years, plant trees; if your plan is for one hundred years, educate children.

—Confucius

School reform efforts, from the first attempt at modernizing schools even to the most recent emphases on outcome-based education and site-based management, have often adopted language that quickly evolved into jargon and then passed into history as the reform movement was abandoned. Is quality learning another example of a movement that will become dated, and then outdated?

While the language of quality has its limitations (educators will perhaps never feel comfortable with *customers* or *outputs* in describing what they do), the concepts of quality learning are timeless because they do not represent a single program or movement. Instead, they provide a framework within which improvement of all kinds can take place. They are not a template to be imitated or applied, but instead represent a way of thinking. Quality learning is not a reform program, as we have emphasized, but a way of seeing all aspects of education as they relate to each other and to their customers.

Building a new house

Quality learning represents a way of seeing. Its language is of vision, purpose, and improvement. It is in this sense theoretical. The theory of quality learning is embodied in the principles that recognize systems (perhaps the most fundamental of the principles), customers, human behavior (including the psychology of learning), and change. Making these principles into concrete realities is the challenge of each organization.

To envision an educational system grounded in these principles provides an opportunity for what Russell Ackoff (1993) calls "idealized redesign." This strategy involves thinking about the system as if there

157

were no system already in place—the kind of thinking home owners would engage in by imagining that their house has burned down and they must start over. They would have an opportunity to change the things they never liked about the original house and to develop new features that were not possible with old constraints. This kind of thinking is useful even if the house does not burn down, because it represents an opportunity to refocus the problem with new thinking. This chapter will offer an opportunity to dream about the new house but then to return to the reality of the situation. We are not starting from scratch, but must renovate what we have. By imagining the ideal school, we can indeed create the schools we want.

What is the ideal classroom? There may be more agreement on this than we realize. Even without a consensus about purpose, for example, many can envision an environment that is active, where students and teachers are engaged in the learning process, and where young people are given support for their learning. A quality classroom, like a quality product or service, is hard to define, but easily recognized. Or as John Guaspari (1985) suggests in the title of his book, *I Know It When I See It*. Some of the classrooms we know already represent this ideal; others demand change.

Theory alone is not enough to bring about change. It must be supported by processes and tools that are consistent with that theory in order to put it into practice. Nonetheless, the theory must provide clear direction for the change. We need to be very sure that we understand the same theory, or no two of us will design the same house even if we have to live in it together.

Processes, though highly individual to school settings, contribute to the sense of purpose that is fostered by system thinking. The processes of learning about dinosaurs, of gaining confidence in speaking and writing, of creating papier-mâché replicas of the Roman Coliseum, of applying formulas to mathematical problems, and of preparing drama productions, all contribute to the purpose of a system of education. This contribution comes about not because of specific content alone, but by virtue of providing opportunities to develop suitable skills of understanding, analyzing, synthesizing, clarifying, and so on. In this sense, it does not really matter whether students understand everything about the Paleozoic Age, for example. It is critical, however, that students know how to find out about the Paleozoic Age, and, of course, how it is related both to dinosaurs and to student life in the twentieth century— and to have some excitement about it, one hopes. It is thinking skills, not the specific content, that characterizes real learning.

Each level of learning provides its own appropriate depth and breadth of understanding, as brain theory suggests. Thus, content directives and must-read book lists cannot be seen as the answer to what ails our schools. If students' interests are aroused, through a sense of purpose; if precision is developed, with the vocabulary and tools necessary for understanding and communication; and if the ability to generalize and apply is fostered, through authentic learning tasks, it makes little difference whether students read *The House of the Seven Gables* or *The Scarlet Letter.* The important outcome is the students' abilities to apply what is learned—ideas, skills, and knowledge—to new situations. These situations include meeting new characters in literature or new people in life, pursuing further reading, and simply living daily life with openness and joy in learning.

Schools of the future

Among those who are trying to "reinvent the future of school" is Seymour Papert, director of the Epistomology and Learning Group at the Massachussetts Institute of Technology (Hill, 1994). Papert points out that while the world has experienced "megachange" in communications, health care, transportation, and recreation, the classroom has evolved very little since the turn of the century. Educators remain largely committed to educational philosophies developed in the nineteenth century and in the early part of this century. Since they are unable to change the system within which they find themselves, individual students—or "yearners" as Papert calls them—and their parents simply find ways to get around schools. Among these methods are home schooling or alternative schools. Teachers, too, find ways to develop learning centers in their classrooms that have little to do with the school community within which they find themselves. It is to be remembered that these approaches represent beginnings; they do not fundamentally change the school system as a whole. Nonetheless, they support the aim of the school, to develop learning.

In assessing reform in school, Papert urges those who share his vision of the future to simply abandon the present system of education and form their own "little schools," characterized by shared vision and "authentic personal beliefs." While this alternative is appealing to many, it is clear that it reflects a deeply shared belief that the public schools cannot really improve, and that the best hope is to build smaller systems of schooling that can be more responsive to students' needs.

We may picture such little schools as isolated units of learning, each with its own purpose. This vision, however, is not necessarily one of fragmentation. Even with much smaller units of schooling, each of which has defined its own vision, a sense of larger system can invigorate these units and give them connectedness to the society within which they operate. Understanding the customer, in the largest meaning of that

term, suggests that all schools ultimately respond to the same customer—students as well as future generations that will depend on current school populations for the leadership and problem-solving skills to
assure survival.

But they'd better hurry. As a high school senior announced on a mi-
crophone at a Global Awareness Day sponsored by AFS Intercultural
Programs in Ohio, "I suddenly realize that if we don't address some of
these [environmental] problems, our children won't even have a *chance*
to solve them." The same observation might be made of our schools,
which are on the brink of tremendous change—even, some would assert, of destruction.

The challenge facing school reformers, then, may be one of accom-
modating specific needs of internal customers within a large framework
of external customers, both present and perhaps especially those of the
future. Generations of private and independent schools have balanced
this accommodation nicely. While they may have been educating students for a particular or specialized need (vocational skills, religious values, or academic concentration), they have, for the most part, not
operated outside the general system of society and the educational system that serves it. Just because students educated in parochial schools,
for example, have had the advantage of the moral and religious training, which they and their families sought, does not mean that they cannot also be prepared for good citizenship in a world that does not share
their religious orientations. Schools can have their own narrowly defined purposes and visions and yet support the purpose and vision of the
large system of education.

When schools recognize that they are all in the business of preparing graduates to function as citizens in large communities with pluralistic values, the relationship of one school to another can be one of
support, not competition. A private school with 100 students can do
quite different things from a public school with 2500, but the reverse is
also true. Quality education prepares students for a world with a variety of threats and challenges, and each type of education and each individual classroom can support this aim.

The school of the future—for that matter, the workplace and the
home of the future—will have an emphasis on technology that we cannot immediately envision. In the same way, schools of the 1930s could
not have foreseen the impact of broadcast media on student learning,
nor, might it be argued, did they adequately prepare their students to
deal with this dramatic change in their lives. Our schools cannot provide or even anticipate precise technological developments of the mid-
twenty-first century. Most cannot afford even the technology that is
currently available. The challenge is to prepare students to critically
evaluate and use whatever technology will be available in their lives.

This is like walking in a dark tunnel, to be sure. But by continuing to prepare students to think and learn, rather than only to do, educational systems will produce graduates who are ready for whatever comes. Like students who attend a school with a specialized purpose, all students must learn to live in environments that do not always mirror their own comfortable experiences. The ideal school will prepare them for this expanded world.

Quality as a framework

Systems thinking, and its understanding of the dynamic needs of customers, support a variety of school models because they identify the interconnectedness of systems. The needs of internal customers do not have to be seen as a source of conflict with those of external customers, for the two can interface positively even within a diverse range of small-school models. The key is in identifying the large system and its purpose, as well as the small unit's contribution to this purpose.

Quality learning, with its framework for seeing schools anew, provides a sense of connectedness among various components of the system of education. It also gives an essential foundation for the necessary interactions between schools and society. As noted in the diagram of a system in chapter 2, customer needs are fundamental to understanding purpose.

It is within this framework that a number of current reforms in education can be placed, demonstrating how quality learning does not contradict or supersede thoughtful changes that have already been made, but indeed places these changes within the system of education and its purpose. Site-based management, for example, represents a potentially powerful strategy to transfer ownership of school issues to schools themselves and to bring decision making close to those directly involved in educational processes. Seeing this approach against larger issues of purpose and vision, variation in systems, and customer needs provides a way of reaffirming purpose while evaluating the specific strategy itself. A question that arises from systems thinking relates to suboptimization: Is the school placing an inordinate number of its resources, for example, into assuring the success of site-based management without understanding how this management contributes to its larger purposes? Any specific strategy, program, or solution can take on a life of its own when it is not placed with a context. Quality learning provides this context.

The network of never-ending contexts is somewhat like a mirror held up to another mirror, the same objects repeatedly reproduced in the two reflected images. Interdependence between the individual component and its larger environment represents an aspect of systems thinking that is particularly vital to schools. In quantum physics, this interdependency is called contextualism; in art, T.S. Eliot observes something like it in "Tradition and the Individual Talent." While the scientific principle of contextualism has been improperly construed to suggest that things have meaning only with respect to their contexts, it seems more accurate to say that things are what they apparently are because of the multiple interactions and relationships that they experience. This is at least how we know them.

Small steps

Within the context of theory, a number of steps can be taken to interact with the present system in order to create a new one. Translating quality theory into concrete reality means recognizing that the individuals in the system cannot change the entire system all at once. When managers of the entire school system are not ready to begin the quality improvement process, however, individual educators can effect change and begin the steps toward improving the system. There must be first steps in any change.

Situations where individual teachers are using quality learning to improve their classrooms even without the support of their leaders are legion. When they are introduced to quality learning principles, educators' frequent response is, "This may make a lot of sense, but my principal [superintendent/board of education/department head] will never support it." It is important to understand that there are ways to introduce this new way of thinking, one person at a time. Concentrating on their own circle of control, teachers can begin to change the system in small increments. Examples of these incremental improvements are easy to find.

- When they must give grades, teachers can minimize the competitive impact of these grades by using alternative assessments and conferences to enhance student opportunities to evaluate their own work and even determine criteria for assigning their own grades.
- Tools of quality management can be adapted for application to classroom use. Cause-and-effect diagrams, flowcharts, histograms, and other analytical tools will reinforce the importance of data in decision making and clarify thought processes. Before students begin a lab experiment, they can create a flowchart of the process; when they study the Civil War, a cause-and-effect di-

agram will help clarify their thinking about the big picture of the war; a language class can create a histogram related to verb usage; and so on.

• Students can be introduced to systems thinking and understanding of variation as they examine classroom processes. This thinking will ultimately become a new way of seeing with respect to other processes in their lives. This is true even in supposedly terrible schools, with problems so complex they defy solution, for it gives students and teachers a sense of control over their own destinies. Knowing about the learning process (metacognition) enfranchises learners and provides them with choices about their learning lives. The approach can be aligned with the curriculum and can provide a sense of integration to otherwise fragmented 50-minute increments of learning. Systems thinking can be integrated into the smallest events; when a child spills a pot of tempera paint in the first-grade classroom, the class can focus on ways to design the system of organizing art supplies so they will be less likely to fall from the edge of a table.

• In small ways and large, teachers can begin to work to transfer the ownership of the learning process to students. It is not hard to imagine students evaluating their own work, reviewing their portfolios, articulating the purpose of particular activities in the classroom, and creating choices within which they can learn. It is already happening, as has been noted.

• Using theory as a framework for processes and tools, teachers can engage students in meaningful activities that reflect sound principles of learning and brain function. Students can be encouraged to understand how they learn when teachers share these principles with them, and students can develop their own methods for demonstrating how well they know something.

• Making decisions on the basis of data rather than on subjective interpretations and perceived information reinforces skills of analysis and promises improved outcomes of decision making at all levels. Remember that "a fact may blossom into a truth," as Thoreau pointed out. Data can lead to information, which can become knowledge, understanding, and ultimately wisdom, as Ackoff asserts (1990).

The list can go on. While quality learning may seem complex because it demands understanding of systems, it is important to see that this understanding applies to the smallest system as well as to the largest. Third-grade students can understand how applying spelling rules can be seen as a system, subject to variation and serving the needs of a customer. Teachers who want to introduce fine art works to a historical study of industrialization understand how this method has purpose. The teachers are able to relate it not only to a goal of learning about industrialization, but also to the ways in which it reinforces learning styles and brain connections.

A useful approach to understanding the impact that quality learning can have on the classroom is to examine the first steps that educators have taken, and to reflect on how these steps represent not just new techniques, but also genuine change in thinking. Teachers in school districts from Texas to Ohio respond to an "I used to . . . now I . . ." framework for the changes they have made.

- "I used to think in terms of remediation; now I understand variation." (High school teacher)

- "I used to insist on finishing the book no matter what; now I focus more deeply on learning." (High school history teacher)

- "I used to give students just one shot at a test; now I allow them to continue learning concepts they missed, and improve their grades." (High school math teacher)

- "I used to use the word *change;* now I use *improve.*" (Superintendent)

- "I used to give all the rules for the semester on the first day of class; now I brainstorm with students about how we will work together." (Sixth-grade teacher)

- "I used to decide on my room arrangement; now I have students do an affinity exercise and nominal group technique to select the best location for things. Instead of my classroom, it's becoming *our* classroom." (Fifth-grade teacher)

- "I used to threaten with grades; now I spend more time in feedback sessions addressed to improvement." (High school science teacher)

- "I used to think I should know how to do everything myself; now I ask my colleagues and students for suggestions." (High school math teacher)

- "I used to be relieved when someone did poorly on my tests, since it validated the difficulty of the exam; now I know that tests are only a way to see what has to happen next." (High school English teacher)

- "I used to keep supplies locked up so that students couldn't get to them unless I distributed them; now I have students who 'own' the supply process." (Fourth-grade teacher)

• "I used to have the art teacher come to my history class and lecture about art from a particular era; now students do this themselves." (High school history teacher)

Imitation won't work

Latching on to any of these before-and-after statements as a way of explaining quality learning is dangerous and inaccurate, of course. Each technique or approach represents behaviors that have been translated by individual teachers from a large concept of the learning process. As noted, imitating what others do without understanding this context will not bring about lasting improvement. Ralph Waldo Emerson (1842) urged this lesson: "Insist on yourself; never imitate." It may be no more important anywhere than it is in education. A Shakespeare will never be made, Emerson emphasized, by simply imitating Shakespeare. Each classroom and school is unique and can create its own approach to quality learning.

At the heart of the improvement process is the plan-do-study-act (PDSA) cycle, introduced in chapter 5. Even the smallest of processes can be approached with this technique. A drama class that is preparing a production can begin by flowcharting the tasks that need to be done, brainstorming about ways in which these tasks can be approached, collecting data about rehearsals, charting progress with respect to memorizing lines, and developing theory about how to improve the process. A school where violence is part of each day's expectations, or where absences preclude learning for many students, may have further to go toward developing the vision of a quality school, but it can begin tiny steps even with these serious problems. For example, while some may think of Mt. Edgecumbe High School in Sitka, Alaska, as a selective program in a bucolic setting where officials can deny admission to many students, it is, in fact, a school for students from cultures that face many of the complexities that are seen in inner-city schools: poverty, lack of parental support, learning disabilities, drug- and alcohol-related problems, and a diverse ethnic makeup. The PDSA cycle and the emphasis on quality learning can improve any learning environment—residential and day programs, and private and public schools with college preparatory and vocational emphases.

To approach the task in small, step-by-step ways requires no additional school district resources or levy support, but it immediately engages students in the learning process. As the drama class proceeds with its preparations, students will monitor and study not only the drama that they are producing, but also the ways in which they are learning it. In a science class, children not only see how the lima bean grows in the soft wet cotton, but also observe and record that growth. And in the final phase of the cycle, after the stage production is over and the set has been struck, the drama students can record the ways in which the process can be standardized. If early-morning rehearsals had better attendance than after-school sessions, that strategy can be adopted for future stage productions. The students' purposes in staging a dramatic production might have included demonstrating their acting and set design skills, interpreting a dramatic work, learning more about characterization, or a variety of other aims that can be accomplished in the process of producing a play. Agreeing on their purpose before launching into the hours of rehearsal that are demanded will give a sense of wholeness to the effort and a vision of the outcome that each participant can hold onto.

Each improvement, when seen within the context of purpose and broad customer needs, leads inexorably to creating a new way to work together to achieve different results. The real measure of learning is how well newly acquired knowledge can be put to use in a new situation. Students are not likely to discover that they need to be able to dissect every frog that they meet on a walk in the woods. But by dissecting the frog in the artificial atmosphere of the classroom laboratory, they can understand "frogness" when they meet it, and know, for example, that the bullfrog on the rock is not a creature to be feared or reviled (or dissected), but instead one to be understood and appreciated. Students can begin to use their knowledge of the frog in new ways—metaphorically, for example, to enrich their communication about a variety of things. The best poems about frogs are undoubtedly rooted in complex understanding about the creatures. In this sense, the laboratory experience of dissection is an authentic learning experience, whose purpose supports the larger one of education.

If students learn history with the clear purpose of understanding the time in which they live, they may be able to apply some of the lessons that history teaches, and even avoid the calamities that recur without this knowledge. When they learn history only for its own sake, or for the purpose of pleasing teachers, such knowledge occurs in a vacuum, with little application to life. How can we expect such students to become responsive, interested citizens who take their voting responsibilities seriously, if their exposure to history and government has taken place in such a vacuum? This is what Thomas Jefferson meant when he noted that an enlightened citizenry is an educated one.

A view of learning

Organizations such as schools have their own identities and purposes, but by responding and contributing to other organizations and to the larger system, they evolve. No system is permanently fixed, for it must exist in a dynamic world with increasingly complex relationships and interdependencies. Schools of the future will not result from single-minded reform, but from careful evolution.

Quality learning provides a framework within which to view the learning process. Since it is not easy to describe the entire framework in only a few words, TQM or *quality learning* becomes a kind of label, used to summarize that framework in general terms, and to distinguish it from other approaches. Let us not be misled by our own need to simplify in this way. Because it represents a new way of thinking, quality learning cannot be encapsulated in an educational acronym nor fully understood outside its fundamental principles. In the last analysis, understanding the theory, process, and tools that are known as quality represents a new way of seeing—one that identifies the rich connections between prior knowledge and new learning, among processes that are in place to deliver learning opportunities, and ultimately with the larger world in which students and teachers live and function.

Notes

Ackoff, Russell L. 1993. Rethinking education. *Journal of Management Consulting* (fall): 4.

———. 1990. *A theory of a system for educators and managers.* Produced by Clare Crawford-Mason. Written by Lloyd Dobyns. 30 min. Films, Inc. Deming Library, tape XXI.

Emerson, Ralph Waldo. [1842] 1950. Self-reliance. In *Selected Writings of Ralph Waldo Emerson,* edited by Brooks Atkinson. New York: Modern Library Editions.

Guaspari, John. 1985. *I know it when I see it: A modern fable about quality.* New York: AMACOM, a division of the American Management Association.

Hill, D. 1994. Professor Papert and his learning machine. *Teacher Magazine* (January): 16–19.

Selected References

Abbott, Edwin A. [1884] 1992. *Flatland: An imaginative mathematical romance.* Reprint. New York: Dover Books.

Ackoff, Russell L. 1993. Rethinking education. *Journal of Management Consulting* (fall): 4.

————. 1990 *A theory of a system for educators and managers.* Produced by Clare Crawford-Mason. Written by Lloyd Dobyns. 30 min. Films, Inc. Deming Library, tape XXI.

Ackoff, R. L., and F. E. Emery. 1972. *On purposeful systems.* Chicago: Aldine-Atherton.

Armstrong, T. 1993. *Seven kinds of smart: Identifying and developing your many intelligences.* New York: Plume/Penguin Books USA.

Baker, M. C. 1955. *Foundations of John Dewey's educational theory.* New York: Atheling Books, Atherton Press.

Ball, M., M. J. Cleary, S. Leddick, C. Schwinn, D. Schwinn, and E. Torres. 1992. *Improvement tools for education (K–12).* Dayton, Ohio: QIP/PQ Systems.

Ball, M., M. J. Cleary, S. Leddick, C. Schwinn, D. Schwinn, and E. Torres. 1991. *Total quality transformation for K–12 education.* Dayton, Ohio: QIP/PQ Systems.

Barker, Joel. 1989. *Discovering the future: The business of paradigms.* Produced and directed by R. J. Christensen, Brad W. Neal, and J. R. Christensen. 40 min. Burnsville, Minn.: Charthouse Learning. Videotape.

Barth, Roland S. 1988. Principals, teachers, and school leadership. *Phi Delta Kappan* (May): 639–642.

Bateson, G. 1979. *Mind and nature: A necessary unity.* New York: Dutton.

Bennis, Warren. 1989. *On becoming a leader.* Reading, Mass.: Addison-Wesley.

Bloom, B., M. Englehart, E. Furst, W. Hill, and D. Krathwohl, eds. 1956. *Taxonomy of educational objectives: The classification of educational goals.* New York: David McKay.

Bruner, Jerome, J. Goodnow, and G.A. Austin. 1967. *A study of thinking: Studies in cognitive growth.* New York: John Wiley & Sons.

Caine, Renata Nummela, and Geoffrey Caine. 1990. Understanding a brain-based approach to learning and teaching. *Educational Leadership* 48, no. 2:66–70.

————. 1991. *Making connections: Teaching and the human brain.* Alexandria, Va.: Association for Supervision and Curriculum Development.

Capra, Fritjof. 1984. *The turning point: Science, society, and the rising culture.* New York: Bantam.

———. 1985. *The tao of physics.* Boston: New Science Library.

Carnevale, A. P., L. J. Gainer, and A. S. Meltzer. 1988. *Workplace basics: The skills employers want.* Washington, D.C.: American Society for Training and Development and the U.S. Department of Labor.

Chall, J. S., and A. F. Mirsky, eds. 1978. *Education and the brain: The 77th yearbook of the national society for the study of education.* Chicago: National Society for the Study of Education. Distributed by University of Chicago Press.

Covey, Stephen R. 1989. *The seven habits of highly effective people: Powerful lessons in personal change.* New York: Simon and Schuster/Fireside Books.

———. 1990. *Principle-centered leadership.* New York: Simon and Schuster/ Fireside Books.

Csikszentmihalyi, Mihaly. 1990. *Flow: Psychology of optimal experience.* New York: Harper & Row.

Deming, W. Edwards. 1986. *Out of the crisis.* Cambridge, Mass.: MIT Center for Advanced Engineering Study.

———. 1993. *The new economics for business, education, and government.* Cambridge, Mass.: MIT Center for Advanced Engineering Study.

Dobyns, Lloyd, and Clare Crawford-Mason. 1991. *Quality or else.* San Francisco: Houghton Mifflin.

Elkind, D. 1981. *The hurried child: Growing up too fast, too soon.* Reading, Mass.: Addison-Wesley.

Epstein, Herman T. 1978. Growth spurts during brain development: Implications for educational policy and practice. In *The 77th yearbook of the national society for the study of education.* Chicago: NSSE. Distributed by University of Chicago Press.

Evans, F. G. 1976. What research says about grading. In *Degrading the grading myths: A primer of alternatives to grades and marks,* edited by S. B. Simon, and J. A. Bellanca. Washington, D.C.: Association for Supervision and Curriculum Development.

Finn, Chester E. Jr. 1991. *We must take charge: Our schools and our future.* New York: Free Press.

Freedman, S., K. A. Klivington, and R. W. Peterson, eds. 1986. *The brain, cognition, and education.* New York: Academic Press/Harcourt Brace Jovanovich.

Gardner, Howard. 1983. *Frames of mind: The theory of multiple intelligences.* New York: Basic Books.

———. 1991. *The unschooled mind: How children think and how schools should teach.* New York: Basic Books.

George, Paul S. 1984. Theory Z and schools: What can we learn from Toyota? *NASSP Bulletin* (May): 76–81.

Glasser, William. 1990. *The quality school: Managing students without coercion.* New York: Harper & Row.

———. 1990. The quality school: What motivates the ants. *Phi Delta Kappan* 71:6 (February): 424–435.

————. 1992. The quality school curriculum. *Phi Delta Kappan* 73, no. 9:690–694.

Gleick, James. 1987. *Chaos: Making a new science.* New York: Viking.

Greenleaf, Robert. 1977. *Servant leadership: A journey into the nature of legitimate power and greatness.* New York: Paulist Press.

Guaspari, John. 1985. *I know it when I see it: A modern fable about quality.* New York: AMACOM, a division of the American Management Association.

Halford, G. S. 1993. *Children's understanding: The development of mental models.* Hilldale, N.J.: Lawrence Erlbaum Associates.

Hargis, Charles H. 1990. *Grades and grading practices. Obstacles to improving education and to helping at-risk students.* Springfield, Ill.: Charles C. Thomas.

Harman, Willis. 1988. *Global mind change.* Indianapolis: Knowledge Systems.

Hart, Leslie. 1975. *How the brain works: A new understanding of human learning, emotion, and thinking.* New York: Basic Books.

Healy, Jane. 1987. *Your child's growing mind: A guide to learning and brain development from birth to adolescence.* Garden City, N.Y.: Doubleday.

————. 1990. *Endangered minds: Why children don't think and what we can do about it.* New York: Touchtone Books/Simon & Schuster.

Hill, D. 1994. Professor Papert and his learning machine. *Teacher Magazine* (January): 16–19.

Jantsch, Erich. 1980. *The self-organizing universe.* New York: Pergamon Press.

Johnson, David W., and Andrew Ahlgren. 1976. Relationship between student attitudes about cooperation and competition and attitudes toward schooling. *Journal of Education Psychology* 68, no. 1:92–102.

Johnson, D. W., and R. T. Johnson. 1991. *Learning together and alone: Cooperative, competitive, and individualistic learning.* 3d ed. Boston: Allyn & Bacon.

Kohn, Alfie. 1986. *No contest: The case against competition.* New York: Houghton Mifflin.

————. 1993. *Punished by rewards.* New York: Houghton Mifflin.

Kume, Hitoshi. 1985. *Statistical methods for quality improvement.* Tokyo: 3A Corporation.

Laszlo, Ervin. 1969. *System, structure, and experience: Toward a scientific theory of mind.* New York: Gordon & Beach Science Publishers.

————. 1972. *The systems view of the world.* New York: George Brazillier.

————. 1974. *A strategy for the future: The systems approach to world order.* New York: George Brazillier.

Leinhardt, Gaea. 1992. What research on learning tells us about teaching. *Educational Leadership* 49, no. 7: 20–24.

Leithwood, Kenneth A. 1992. The move toward transformational leadership. *Educational Leadership* 49, no. 5: 8–12.

Lewin, Kurt. 1989. *The power of the situation.* The Developments in Psychology series. Senior Producer Tug Yourglad. Director Kim Story. 30 min. Videotape.

Lewis Carroll's Alice's Adventures in Wonderland. The Pennyroyal Edition. 1982. Designed and illustrated by Barry Moser. Berkeley, Calif.: University of California Press.

MacLean, P. D. 1978. A mind of three minds: Educating the triune brain. In *The 77th yearbook of the national society for the study of education.* Chicago: NSSE. Distributed by University of Chicago Press.

Markova, D. 1992. *How your child is smart: A life-changing approach to learning.* Berkeley, Calif.: Conari Press.

Merton, Robert K. 1968. The self-fulfilling prophecy. In *Social theory and structure,* edited by Robert K. Merton. New York: Free Press.

Miller, L. M. 1984. *American spirit: Visions of a new corporate culture.* New York: Warner Books.

National Council for Effective Schools Research and Development. 1991. Authentic assessment. *Focus on Change* (Madison: Wisconsin Center for Education Research) (March): 1.

Nummela, Renate, and T. Rosengran. 1986. What's happening in students' brains may redefine teaching. *Educational Leadership* 43, no. 8: 49–53.

Ornstein, R. 1986. *Multimind.* Boston: Houghton Mifflin.

Ornstein, R., and R. F. Thompson. 1982. *The amazing brain.* Boston: Houghton Mifflin.

Papert, Seymour. 1980. *Mindstorms: Children, computers, and powerful ideas.* New York: Basic Books.

Paulson, F. L., P. R. Paulson, and C. A. Meyer. 1991. What makes a portfolio a portfolio? *Educational Leadership* 48, no. 5: 60–63.

Perrone, Vito, ed. 1991. *Expanding student assessment.* Alexandria, Va.: Association for Supervision and Curriculum Development.

Phelan, P., A. L. Davidson, and H. T. Cao. 1992. Speaking up: Students' perspectives on school. *Phi Delta Kappan* 73, no. 9:695–704.

Piaget, J. 1952. *The origins of intelligence in children.* Translated by M. Cook. New York: International Universities Press.

———. 1969. *The psychology of intelligence.* Translated by M. Piercy, and D. E. Berlyne. Totowa, N.Y.: Littlefield, Adams, and Company.

———. 1975. *The development of thought: Equilibrium of cognitive structures.* New York: Viking.

Prigogine, I., and I. Stengers. 1984. *Order out of chaos: Man's dialogue with nature.* New York: Bantam.

Reich, Robert. 1983. *The next American frontier.* New York: Time Books.

Restak, R. 1984. *The brain.* Toronto: Bantam.

Rhodes, L. A. 1990. Why quality is within our grasp . . . If we reach. *The School Administrator* 47, no. 10:31–34.

———. 1992. On the road to quality. *Educational Leadership* 49, no. 6: 76–80.

Sagan, Carl. 1977. *The dragons of Eden: Speculations on the evolution of human intelligence.* New York: Random House.

Sarason, S. B. 1990. *The predictable failure of educational reform.* San Francisco: Jossey-Bass.

Scherkenbach, W. W. 1986. *The Deming route to quality and productivity.* Washington, D.C.: CEEPress.

Senge, Peter. 1990. The leader's new work: Building learning organizations. *Sloan Management Review* (Reprint series 32): 1.

———. 1990. *The fifth discipline: The art and practice of the learning organization.* New York: Doubleday.

Senge, Peter, C. Roberts, R. Ross, B. Smith, and A. Kleiner. 1994. *The fifth discipline fieldbook: Strategies and tools for building a learning organization.* New York: CurrencyDoubleday.

Slavin, R. 1983. *Cooperative learning.* New York: Longman.

Springer, S. P., and G. Deutsch. 1981. *Left brain, right brain.* New York: W.H. Freeman and Company.

Strom, R. D. 1971. *Teachers and the learning process.* Englewood Cliffs, N.J.: Prentice Hall.

Swimme, Brian., and Thomas Berry. 1992. *The universe story.* San Francisco: HarperSan Francisco, a division of HarperCollins Publishers.

Theobald, R. 1982. *Avoiding 1984: Moving toward interdependence.* Chicago: Swallow Press.

———. 1987. *The rapids of change.* Indianapolis: Knowledge Systems.

———. 1992. *Turning the century.* Indianapolis: Knowledge Systems.

Tribus, Myron. 1988. *Quality first: Selected papers on quality and productivity.* Washington, D.C.: National Society of Professional Engineers.

Vaill, Peter. 1989. *Managing as a performing art.* San Francisco: Jossey-Bass.

Von Bertalanffry, Ludwig. 1968. *General system theory.* New York: George Brazillier.

Werner, Heinz. 1957. The concept of development from a comparative and organismic point of view. In *Developmental processes: Heinz Werner's selected writings,* edited by S. S. Barten, and M. B. Franklin. New York: International Universities Press.

Wheatley, Margaret J. 1992. *Leadership and the new science: Learning about organizations from an orderly universe.* San Francisco: Barrett-Koehler Publishers.

Wheeler, D. J. 1993. *Understanding variation: The key to managing chaos.* Knoxville, Tenn. SPC Press.

Whitehead, Alfred North. 1929. *The aims of education and other essays.* New York: Macmillan.

Zohar, D. 1990. *The quantum self: Human nature and consciousness defined by the new physics.* New York: William Morrow & Company.

Glossary of Selected Tools and Terms

Illustrations are provided for recognition purposes only. See text reference for more complete descriptions.

Affinity diagram   A tool that provides a way to organize the output of brainstorming sessions by grouping and categorizing it for further analysis. Categories are based on shared characteristics and items are generated either by brainstorming or by the Crawford slip method.

Brainstorming   A tool for generating a great number of ideas from a group. In response to a question or selected issue, every particpant provides his or her input; one person speaks at a time, until no further ideas are generated by the group.

Cause-and-effect chart   Sometimes known as a fishbone diagram or Ishikawa chart after the Japanese statistician Kaoru Ishikawa, this tool provides a way to generate and categorize causes for a given effect.

Common causes   After gathering data and charting the data points (see *control chart*), these are the causes of variation that are universal and ordinary, or inherent in the system, rather than created by unusual circumstances (see *special cause*). Common causes of variation can be altered only by changing the system.

Consensogram (Langford consensogram)   A tool used to survey an entire group's response to a specific question, usually in the form of a percentage response about commitment, effort, and so on. (Example: "How confident do you feel about your

Affinity diagram

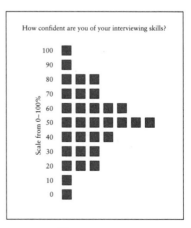

Consensogram

175

interviewing skills at this point in the class?" A student will respond in a percentage form on a small sticky note that can be posted with other students' responses, giving a profile of class confidence levels.)

Constancy of purpose A clearly articulated and consistent sense of the aim of a system. For improvement to come about, everyone in the system must have constancy of purpose, one of W. Edwards Deming's 14 points.

Control chart A statistical tool useful for plotting data over time in order to determine whether a system is stable or not by evaluating its variation. (See *common cause* and *special cause*.) Also called variables chart.

Control limits After gathering data and recording data points on a control chart, these limits, or lines, are calculated using a simple formula. They are not imposed from

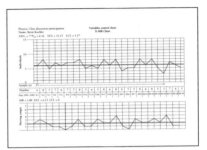

Control chart

without, but generated by the data. The formulas for variables data are as follows:

$$\overline{X} = \frac{\Sigma X}{n} \qquad UCL_x = \overline{X} + (2.66 \times \overline{R}) \qquad UCL_R = \overline{R} \times D_3$$

$$\overline{R} = \frac{\Sigma R}{n-1} \qquad LCL_x = \overline{X} - (2.66 \times \overline{R}) \qquad LCL_R = \overline{R} \times D_4$$

Competency matrix (or learning competency matrix) A charting technique used to break down topic or subject areas into steps for accomplishing a specific learning outcome. Using Bloom's taxonomy, the matrix identifies tasks, knowledge levels, and depth of understanding of each subject area, so that students and teachers can evaluate competency with a given skill or concept.

Cooperative learning A classroom approach that emphasizes teamwork and collaboration rather than individual performance and competition. Teams work toward a common learning opportunity, supporting each other in order to achieve a common vision.

Crawford slip process An alternative to the brainstorming tool; instead of generating ideas aloud, participants record them on small slips of paper, with one idea per slip. This tool minimizes influences from the group and reduces fear when there is danger that this might exist in a group.

Customer One who derives benefit from any process. Internal customers are those within the system who gain from its processes; external customers are those who receive the benefit of a system but are not directly involved in its processes.

Customer expectations Those aspects of a system that its customers have come to regard as givens. These expectations can be measured, unlike customer needs, which cannot be measured, though they can be assessed.

Customer needs The benefit that a customer requires from a system. Needs may be expressed or implied, and form the basis for improvement that ultimately creates customer expectations.

Facilitator One who supports a group or individual process by removing barriers. A learning facilitator (a teacher, for example) will help student learning by providing an environment, materials, information, and other resources that are required for the learning process. A group facilitator may elect to be outside the process (such as in a brainstorming process), in order to facilitate its smooth operation.

Flowchart A graphic portrayal of a process, showing the steps that are involved in that process and their relationship to one another. A process flowchart shows the steps, in time order; a deployment flowchart includes a people coordinate to illustrate who is responsible for each step in the process.

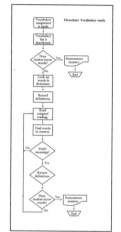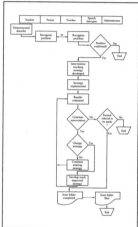

Flowcharts

Force field analysis A method of visually organizing items that tend to drive a change forward and those that work to restrain it. Using this tool in problem solving, teams can choose to increase the driving forces or diminish the restraining forces. This tool was originally developed by psychologist Kurt Lewin.

Histogram or bar chart A tool that illustrates collected data for analyzing frequency of occurrence. This tool gives additional information about a system so that it can be improved on the basis of data rather than mere whim.

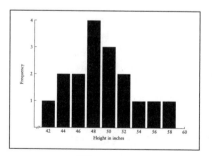

Histogram

Metacognition Consciousness or awareness of the thinking and learning process itself and of the ways in which students learn best; knowing what one knows.

Nominal group technique An approach to problem solving that helps teams to make decisions. A list of items generated by brainstorming is considered against agreed-upon decision criteria, with team members selecting from four to eight ideas that meet these criteria and, in their opinions, should be considered.

Operational definition   Clear and highly specific explanation of terms that are used in the improvement process. In order to pursue that process, everyone involved must have the same understanding of the meanings of these terms.

Optimization   Deriving the best possible outcome from a system by focusing on the entire system rather than only its parts. Rendering a system fully effective demands an understanding of system purpose and customer needs as well as an appreciation of variation.

Out of control   A system is said to be statistically out of control when data points fall outside statistically calculated control charts; when there is a run of seven points or more that are either above or below the center line; when a run of data points goes in the same direction (up or down); or when data patterns appear too close or too far from the average. Analysis is based on the data itself, not on subjective judgment.

PDSA cycle   Statistician Walter Shewhart's description of the improvement cycle, emphasized by W. Edwards Deming. The four stages of plan, do, study, and act are essential to continuous improvement success, and are the basis for a seven-step improvement process that is characterized by improvement efforts. (The seven steps are (1) defining the system; (2) assessing the current situation; (3) analyzing causes; (4) trying out an improvement theory; (5) studying the results; (6) standardizing the improvement; and (7) planning for continuous improvement.)

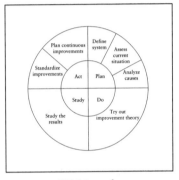

PDSA cycle

Pareto diagram   Like a histogram, this can also be considered a type of bar chart. It provides additional information, however, by ranking related items with respect to frequency of occurrence, from greatest to least. This helps to separate items that are significant in terms of number of occurrences from those that are less significant. A cumulative percentage line appears above the bars. This tool was developed by Italian economist Vilfredo Pareto.

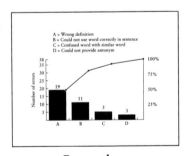

Pareto chart

Portfolio   An alternative method of assessing student work by collecting samples of written expression or artwork for review with students. The method provides a basis for students, teachers, and parents to see progress, identify best work, and develop pride in learning.

Purpose The aim of a system or of a system improvement. Purpose is determined through leadership and consensus, and is closely related to the needs and expectations of the customers of the system.

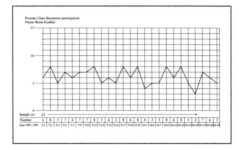

Run chart

Run chart A statistical tool that records data chronologically. Observations are entered on a chart over a period of time in order to observe a system's behavior with respect to trends and patterns. After collecting data over a sufficient period of time, a control chart can be constructed that provides additional information about the system.

Self-managed groups Teams or groups of people who function without the need for external direction. Students who work in groups to support and facilitate each other's learning, or teachers working toward solving a common problem, are examples of this kind of teamwork.

Special causes Variation that occurs because of a unique situation or unpredicable occurrence. Variation that is created by factors that are universal to the system are considered common causes.

Statistical process control (SPC) The use of data and statistical tools to monitor processes over time. SPC helps to prevent problems in a system rather than merely detecting those that are occurring.

Suboptimization A phenomenon that occurs when attention or resources are diverted to a subsystem or a part of a system without considering the effect that will be derived by the system as a whole.

Subsystem A component of a larger system, to which the same understandings of customer, purpose, and variation apply. Subsystems contribute to the purpose of the larger system of which they are parts, even though they may have specifically defined purposes of their own.

System A collection of processes and people that are aligned toward serving a common purpose or aim. A system includes inputs, outputs, feedback mechanisms, and customers. Laszlo defined a system as a collection of parts with an identifiable set of internal relationships as well as identifiable external relationships to other systems.

Tampering Making changes in a system without benefit of adequate data, or responding to special causes as if they were common causes.

Taxon learning Learning that depends on taxon memory, consisting of items that do not depend on specific physical contexts. Information is placed in taxon memory through memorization and practice, and is often associated with rote learning processes and physical learning (like riding a bike). Taxon memory includes information or skills that can be recalled and used with little reference to meaning.

Total quality management   A way of managing systems that includes an emphasis on understanding systems, variation, and customer needs and a focus on making improvement after collecting data and analyzing responses to what is suggested by that data. TQM utilizes statistical and problem-solving tools to bring about planned change and continuous improvement in a system.

Variation   A common characteristic of systems. Variation can be analyzed by means of appropriate statistical tools so that it can be reduced and improvement can ensue. Variation may be due to common or special causes.

Index